SAFE PREPARED EQUIPPED

Preparedness as a vital life skill

DISCLAIMER

Project SPE offers information and is designed for educational purposes only. You should not rely on this information as a substitute for, nor does it replace, professional medical advice, diagnosis or treatment.

The content on this book is provided as general information only. Any action taken as a result of information, analysis, or advertisement on this document is ultimately the responsibility of the reader.

You are responsible for your own actions.

Although the publisher and the author have made every effort to ensure that the information in this book was correct at press time and while this publication is designed to provide accurate information in regard to the subject matter covered, the publisher and the author assume no responsibility for errors, inaccuracies, omissions, or any other inconsistencies herein and hereby disclaim any liability to any party for any loss, damage, or disruption caused by errors or omissions, whether such errors or omissions result from negligence, accident, or any other cause.

iii

THE POCKET PREP

You have in your hand a comprehensive set of flashcards designed to enhance your emergency preparedness and equip you with essential tips for various crisis situations. From natural disasters to medical emergencies, Project SPE ensures you're ready for any challenge life throws your way.

This book aims to empower you with the skills and knowledge to prepare for and manage emergencies specific to your daily environment and navigate life's uncertainties with confidence.

Stay prepared anywhere, anytime with the Pocket Prep. This compact guide fits easily into your pocket, everyday carry bag, backpack, or glove compartment, providing instant access to vital educational resources for emergency situations.

Safe, Prepared, Equipped: three steps to emergency readiness.

About the author: With over two decades in crisis and risk management, Franck Amato's credentials are undeniable. As a former Special Forces officer, surgical hospital executive director, and consultant for international institutions, he brings a unique perspective on handling emergencies.

Franck's extensive knowledge and hands-on experience are the backbone of Project SPE's practical approach to emergency preparedness. Trust his expertise to keep you and your loved ones safe.

As a husband, father, world traveler, and entrepreneur, Franck understands the human toll and potential in any crisis. He founded Project SPE to harness that potential—for resilience, leadership, and confidence—helping individuals and communities overcome challenges and emerge stronger.

SPEro
A combination of SPE — safe, prepared, equipped — with hero. The person who is in charge of the emergency planning for their household, the "hero" of the family.

CONTENT

EQUIPPED

SAFE

PERSONAL ASSESSMENT

Understanding the specific type of disaster that could affect your residential and work area, along with the potential impacts on your daily life, is crucial.

While some of these questions may seem obvious, it is vital to have a clear understanding of your situation and be able to communicate it effectively with first responders during an emergency.

Completing this assessment will assist you in customizing your emergency plan according to your individual needs and requirements.

HOUSEHOLD

- How many members are there within your household?
- How old are they?
- What languages do they speak?
- What are their specific dietary needs?
- What are their specific medical needs?
- Do any of them have a specific disability?

PETS

- How many are there?
- What type of pet?
- What are their specific dietary needs?
- What are their specific medical needs?

HOUSING

- What type of residence do you inhabit (house or apartment)?
- If it's an apartment, on which floor are you located?
- What safety equipment do you have in your living space (smoke alarms, carbon monoxide alarms, extinguisher)?
- Where are the emergency exits?
- Make sure you know where your electricity breakers, gas line valves, and water valves are located and how to operate them (Note that if you turn off the gas, only a qualified professional should restore it; never attempt to do it yourself).

ENVIRONMENT

- What is your living and working environment (Urban/rural/coastline/mountain/forest)?
- What are the potential risks associated with these environments?
- What are the annual weather patterns and their effects on your daily life?
- What transportation options are available, including roads and public transportation?
- What are the nearest safety and security resources, such as fire stations, police stations, hospitals, public facilities, and designated shelters in case of emergencies?

PERSONAL INFORMATION

Having basic personal information, such as your name, contact information, and medical condition, within your everyday carry emergency kit is crucial for several reasons:

Identification in an emergency: In case you are incapacitated or unable to communicate, first responders or others can quickly identify you and contact your loved ones or medical professionals. This ensures that you receive timely and appropriate care.

Medical Information: If you have specific medical conditions, allergies, or are on medication, this information can be vital in an emergency. First responders can adjust their treatment to avoid complications and ensure your safety.

Communication: Your contact information allows others to reach your emergency contacts if needed. This is particularly important if you are in a situation where you cannot communicate or if you need someone to be informed about your situation quickly.

It's also a good idea for your kids to carry their own personal information in their emergency kits, especially if they are old enough to understand the importance of it.

PERSONAL INFORMATION

Name: ....

Address: ....

....

....

Phone: ....

Emergency contacts:

....

....

Out-of-town contact: ....

....

Languages spoken:

....

Health information: Blood type: ....

Medication: ....

....

Allergies: ....

....

....

ALERTS AND WARNINGS

Receiving alerts and staying updated with information about ongoing or upcoming emergencies is crucial for making decisions.

Include a compilation of alert systems in your emergency plan, ensuring easy access when needed. Bear in mind that in the absence of official information, rumors and speculation tend to fill the void. It's essential to identify trustworthy sources and verify information before sharing.

WIRELESS EMERGENCY ALERTS [WEAs]

- WEA messages look like a regular text. The message will show the type and time of the alert, action you should take, and the agency issuing the alert.
- Most modern phones are WEAs compatible (if you are not sure about yours, check with your provider).
- You don't need to download any application to receive WEAs alerts.
- WEAs have a unique tone and vibration.
- You will never be charged for this service.
- If you are on a phone call when a WEA is sent, the message will be delayed until you finish your call.
- WEAs are not affected by network congestion.
- The system does not track your location or your phone number. The alerts are sent to any devices in a given area.

There are three types of warnings that will trigger a Wireless Emergency Alert (WEA).

- **Presidential Alerts** are a special class of alerts issued by the U.S. President for a nationwide emergency.
- **Imminent threat Alerts** are usually issued by the National Weather Service for natural or human-made disasters that are current or emerging.
- **America's Missing or Broadcast Emergency Response (AMBER) Alerts** are urgent bulletins issued by law enforcement in child-abduction cases.

NOAA WEATHER RADIO ALL HAZARDS
[NWR]

- The NWR network covers all 50 states, adjacent coastal waters, Puerto Rico, the U.S. Virgin Islands, and the U.S. Pacific Territories.
- The NWR broadcasts warnings, watches, advisories,
- forecasts, general weather information, and other hazard information 24 hours a day, 7 days a week.
- Weather messages are generally repeated every 4 to 10 minutes, with regular updates occurring every 1 to 3 hours, or more frequently according to the situation.
- Emergency broadcasts can't be received on standard AM/FM radios. Instead, they use 7 specific VHF frequencies between 162.400 MHz and 162.550 MHz.
- When selecting a radio, ensure it can receive Weather Bands (WB) frequencies.
- Make sure to check your local frequency on the National
- Weather Service's website and have it programmed or noted on your radio.
- If mobile and internet networks are down, have a crank or solar powered radio to stay informed.

FIRST AID BASICS

PROVIDING FIRST AID

THE 3 C'S RULE

CHECK   Make sure the scene is safe before approaching. Then check the victim to identify the problem.

CALL   Call 911

If you ask someone to get help, be specific: "please call 911" rather than "go get help".

CARE   Introduce yourself (first name). Explain that you know first aid and get permission to treat the victim.

STAY CALM

- A calm mind allows for clear thinking and effective decision-making.
- Remaining calm helps reassure the injured person and provide emotional support.
- Staying calm helps manage stress levels for the person receiving assistance and avoid panic among bystanders and those directly involved.

Do not move an injured person unless it is absolutely necessary (in case of further danger).

CALLING 911 FOR HELP

THE 3 W'S RULE

WHO   Give your name, and the phone number you are calling from.

WHAT   Explain the situation: what do you see, how many people are hurt, what are their injuries.

WHERE Give your exact location: the name of the street or a recognizable landmark.

Never hang up until the operator tells you to.

PROTECTIVE MEASURES WHEN PROVIDING FIRST AID

- Consider all blood as if it contains germs and avoid using your bare hands to stop bleeding, use a protective barrier such as latex-free disposable gloves.
- If you have any cuts on your hands, cover them with a bandage.
- If you don't have gloves, wash your hands or use hand sanitizer before touching the victim.
- Always wash your hands and other exposed skin after treating the victim.

HEAT RELATED ILLNESS

Healthy internal body temperature: between 98°F (37°C) and 100°F (37.8°C). Heat-related illnesses happen when the body is not able to properly cool itself. While sweating is the usual mechanism for cooling the body, in extreme heat conditions, this might not be enough.

Certain populations, such as young children, infants, older adults, pregnant women and individuals with chronic medical conditions, are more susceptible to heat-related issues.

Risk-increasing factors include:

- Elevated humidity levels.
- Dehydration.
- Consumption of alcohol.
- Obesity.
- Sunburn.
- Some medical conditions like poor blood circulation, heart disease.
- Some prescription drugs.

Common heat related illness include:
- Heat cramps
- Heat exhaustion
- Heat stroke

 Healthy internal body temperature: between 98°F (37°C) and 100°F (37.8°C).

HEAT CRAMPS

SYMPTOMS INCLUDE:

- Heavy sweating.
- Muscle spasms occurring in the stomach, arms, or legs.

TREATMENT:

- Stop physical activity.
- Move the victim's body to a cool and well-ventilated place.
- Remove excess clothing and utilize cool compresses on the forehead and chest.
- Provide water, slightly salty beverages (to replace lost electrolytes) or sport drinks. *
- Gently stretch any muscles that are cramping.
- Get medical assistance if cramps last more than one hour or if the victim has a heart condition.

* *Electrolytes are crucial minerals like sodium, potassium, magnesium, and chloride that play a vital role in supporting the body's ability to absorb water.*

HEAT EXHAUSTION

SYMPTOMS INCLUDE:

- Exhaustion.
- Cool, moist, pale, or flushed skin.
- Heavy sweating.
- Headache.
- Nausea or vomiting.
- Dizziness.
- Fainting.

TREATMENT:

- Stop physical activity.
- Move the victim's body to a cool and well-ventilated place.
- Remove excess clothing and utilizing cool compresses.
- Provide water, slightly salty beverages (to replace lost electrolytes) or sport drinks. Electrolytes are crucial minerals like sodium, potassium, magnesium, and chloride that play a vital role in supporting the body's ability to absorb water.
- Mist them with water and blow air across their bodies.
- Get medical assistance if symptoms get worse or last more than one hour.

 If left untreated, heat exhaustion will develop into heat stroke.

HEAT STROKE

SYMPTOMS INCLUDE:

- High body temperature.
- Hot, red skin.
- Lack of sweat.
- Rapid pulse.
- Confusion.
- Dizziness.
- Fainting.

TREATMENT:

- Heat stroke is a medical emergency, call 911.
- To cool down the body, remove excess clothing and utilize cool compresses or showers.
- Apply ice packs to the neck, groin and armpits (not directly on the skin, wrap it in a dry cloth).
- Avoid giving any medications.
- Have the victim drink water slowly (to avoid vomiting).

 In any case, if you are uncertain about the signs of heat related illness or about what to do, call 911.

HYPOTHERMIA

Hypothermia happens when your body temperature drops below 95°F or 35°C (normal body temperature is about 98.6°F or 37°C). Hypothermia is caused by prolonged exposure to very cold temperatures or if a person is wet (from rain, snow, sweat or immersion in cold water) and becomes chilled.

 Hypothermia is a medical emergency, left untreated, hypothermia can lead to cardiac arrest and death.

SOME PEOPLE ARE AT A HIGHER RISK

- Babies lose body heat more easily than adults, and don't have the energy reserve to shiver (a natural way to increase body heat).
- Children are physically more active than adults
- (proportionally) and use more body calories, as such they may not realize they are cold when playing outside.
- Elderly people gradually lose the ability to control body temperature.
- Alcohol or drugs can affect a person's ability to feel cold. It also affects blood flow and increases body heat loss.
- Individuals taking certain medications (including sedatives, anesthetics, opioids) may be more susceptible to cold temperature.

COMMON SIGNS AND SYMPTOMS

For adults:

- Shivering.
- Exhaustion.
- Confusion, poor judgment, slurred speech
- Loss of movement coordination.
- Drowsiness.
- Pale skin color.
- Abnormal heart rhythm.
- Muscle stiffness.

Additionally for children:

- Bright red, cold skin.
- Very low energy.

TREATMENT

- Move to a warm, dry place.
- Remove wet clothing.
- Dry the victim's skin if wet.
- Cover up with dry clothing or a blanket, hat and socks.
- Warm the abdomen first.
- Don't apply hot packs directly to the skin.
- Providing warm liquids to a victim to drink, ensuring they are not too hot.

 In any case, if you are uncertain about the signs of hypothermia or about what to do, call 911.

FROSTBITE

Frostbite is a condition that occurs when the skin freezes upon exposure to cold weather or cold water. It typically affects body extremities, such as fingers, toes, ears, and the nose, where blood flow is lower.

3 STAGES OF FROSTBITE

Frostnip: In the initial stages of frostbite, the affected skin may feel cold and numb, displaying a coloration that can be either red or pale. The skin damage is generally still temporary.

Surface frostbite: As frostbite progresses, the water within the skin starts to freeze, leading to potential swelling and the formation of blisters. At this stage, medical treatment becomes necessary to address the severity of the condition.

Severe (deep) frostbite: In advanced stages of frostbite, exposed areas can become completely numb and insensitive as the lower layers of the skin freeze. This represents a more severe and critical condition requiring immediate medical attention.

 In any case, if you are uncertain about the signs of frostbite or about what to do, call 911.

FROSTBITE SYMPTOMS

- Numbness.
- Pain in the exposed skin area.
- Swelling or blisters.
- Loss of coordinated movements.
- Redness (for frostnip).
- Pale color skin, unusually firm (for surface frostbite).
- Blackened skin (for severe frostbite).

FROSTBITE TREATMENT

- Use caution when providing treatment as individuals
- experiencing frostbite may exhibit numbness in the
- affected skin and potential tissue damage.
- Seek medical attention as soon as possible.
- Get them into a warm room or shelter.
- Remove any wet clothing.
- Never rub or massage areas with frostbite.
- Remove any jewelry from the affected area because it may swell.
- Soak the frostbitten area in warm water (around 100°F or 38°C) until the skin feels soft again.
- Do not use hot sources like a fireplace, heat lamp, or stove for warming.
- Loosely dress the area with dry, sterile bandages. If the fingers or toes are frostbitten, place gauze between them to avoid rubbing and pressure.
- Unless necessary, do not let them stand or walk on feet or toes with frostbite.

WATER NEEDS

DRINKABLE WATER

Ensure that your family consistently has access to potable water under any circumstances. Store water in your residence, vehicle, and workplace, and keep readily available bottles in emergency kits, including those for your children and pets.

As a general rule, for healthy people living in temperate climates, consider the daily fluid needs in the chart below:

Age range	Gender	Daily need (cup/day)
Children		
4 to 8 yo	Girls and boys	7 (1.7 liters)
9 to 13 yo	Girls	9 (2.2 liters)
	Boys	10 (2.4 liters)
14 to 18 yo	Girls	10 (2.4 liters)
	Boys	14 (3.3 liters)
Adults		
	Women	11.5 (2.7 liters)
	Men	15.5 (3,7 liters)

While water is vital for good health, individual hydration needs can differ based on various factors such as health status, physical conditions, weight, level of physical activity, and environmental factors like weather conditions and altitude.

Notably, at altitudes above 5000 feet, your body works harder, your respiration rate goes up, and you lose water faster than you would at sea level.

DEHYDRATION

Lack of water can quickly lead to dehydration, a condition that occurs when more water and fluids leave your body than enter it. Even mild dehydration can make you tired.

Warning signs of dehydration include headache, fatigue, muscle weakness, low blood pressure, dizziness, confusion, or nausea.

Severe dehydration includes extreme thirst, lack of sweating, convulsions, fainting, heart failure, rapid and weak breathing and eventually death.

People at a higher risk of dehydration include infants and children, elderly, sick people or suffering from a chronic illness.

 In any case, if you are uncertain about the signs of dehydration or about what to do, call 911.

24

SOURCES OF WATER AT HOME

Water is crucial for survival and comfort; it should be prioritized for drinking and cooking over other uses.

 Always ensure that any water you collect is safe and free from contaminants before using it for consumption.

The first thing you need to know is where your incoming water valve is. In the event of a warning, reports of broken sewage lines, or any potential sources of water contamination — especially after an earthquake — it is crucial to shut off the incoming water valve before opening any faucets in your house.

HOT WATER TANK

Home water heater tanks typically hold 40 to 75 gallons of clean water. To prevent potential contamination from the public water network, it's advisable to shut off the water supply line to the heater, located at the top of the tank.

Adjust the water heater temperature to a range between 130 and 140 degrees Fahrenheit (55 to 60 degrees Celsius).

Ensure the gas or electricity to the water tank is turned off, and wait for the water to cool down. Open the pressure relief valve at the top of the tank and turn on the drain valve at the bottom. Do not restore electricity or gas until the tank is refilled.

HOME WATER PIPES

Water is held under pressure in the pipes and is literally waiting behind the faucet valve.

To utilize the remaining water in your home pipes, follow these steps: turn on the faucet at the highest level in your house to let air into the plumbing system and create natural pressure, then turn on the faucet at the lowest level to collect the water. By doing this, you should be able to collect an additional gallon of water (for a one-story house).

FREEZER

Ice cubes from your freezer are obviously a water source safe to drink. You can also collect the built-up ice inside, which can be an indicator that the freezer drain might be clogged, depending on how clean your freezer is.

TOILET TANK (NOT THE BOWL!)

It might sound odd, but your toilet tank is another source of water you can use. If no cleaning product is being used in the tank, it will provide a couple of gallons of clean water.

Pre-1982 toilets hold 5 to 7 gallons, toilets between 1982 and 1993 hold around 3.5 gallons, and newer ones hold 1.6 gallons.

RAIN WATER

If you have a rainwater collection system or are improvising one with tarp, duct tape, and containers, you will have access to an additional source of water. It's important to note that this water might not be safe to drink, depending on the collection method and air pollution. Ensure proper treatment before use.

CANNED FRUITS AND VEGETABLES

Canned vegetables and fruit contain water that can be consumed, unless they are packed in brine (brine is a liquid mixture of water and salt that is sometimes used as a preserving agent or for flavoring, if canned items are packed in brine, it means they are immersed in a salty solution).

 "Clean water" doesn't necessarily mean safe to drink. If you collect water from these unconventional emergency sources, always ensure to treat it first before using it for drinking, cooking, or even brushing your teeth.

While it's possible to treat water from these sources, it is advisable not to consume it. Instead, use it for sanitation purposes such as personal hygiene and toilet flushing.

GARDEN HOSE

Some water may be sitting in your garden hose, and in addition to bacteria, mold, and other microorganisms, the heat from the sun can enhance the leaching of chemicals from the PVC into the water.

SWIMMING POOL AND SPA

Due to the presence of chemicals, including chlorine, in pool water and spa, it is not recommended for safe human consumption.

WATERBED

Fungicides and other chemicals in the water make it unsafe for drinking.

CONDENSATION FROM AN AIR CONDITIONING SYSTEM OR A DEHUMIDIFIER

According to the Environmental Protection Agency, stagnant condensate can be contaminated by organic substances, including mold, mildew, and algae. Additionally, it may contain metal residues such as lead from the component parts of the device.

ALWAYS CONSIDER FLOOD WATER UNSAFE

During floods resulting from heavy rains, snowmelt, high river levels, and high tides, water meets various contaminants (sewage, fuel, animal waste, and chemicals from industrial facilities. If you have a private drinking water well that has been impacted, it may have been contaminated with pollutants carried in the floodwater.

FLOODED WELL

Refrain from using its water for personal consumption unless the well has been properly disinfected and tested for drinking safety.

You can find information online about "well shock" and "well chlorination shocking" methods, or you can seek assistance from a professional.

DRINKING SEA WATER CAN BE DEADLY

The human body typically eliminates excess salt by producing urine through the kidneys. However, if you were to drink seawater, your body would need to expel more water through urine than you consumed to rid itself of the elevated salt content.

While humans can safely ingest small amounts of salt as part of their daily diet, the concentration of salt in seawater far exceeds what the human body can effectively process.

Freshwater is essential for diluting the salt, allowing the kidneys to function properly. Consuming seawater would result in increased thirst, dehydration, and, in extreme cases, can quickly become a life-threatening situation.

UTILITIES SHUT OFF

Make sure you and your household know where your electricity breakers, gas, and water valves are located and how to operate them.

GAS

A natural gas leak not only increases the potential for fire but also elevates the danger of carbon monoxide poisoning.

Shut off the gas only if:
- you smell gas odor or hear a blowing sound from any pipes or appliances, or
- you notice a broken or disconnected pipe, or
- the meter is spinning quickly (potential leak), or
- your house has slid off its foundation (after a natural disaster).

If you notice or suspect a gas leak:
- open a window,
- evacuate everyone immediately (upwind location),
- do not use matches, lighter, any open flame appliances or tool, electrical switches (they can cause sparks),
- turn off the gas using a wrench to turn the valve one-quarter so that it is perpendicular to the pipe,
- when you are in a safe location, call your gas company.

Don't turn the gas back on yourself, call a qualified professional to do it.

 Place a wrench next to the gas valve to be able to turn it. If it is frozen, call your gas provider to have it fixed or replaced.

ELECTRICITY

Shut off electricity in case of:

- an electrical fire (appliance, wires, motors), or
- flooding, or
- broken or frayed electrical cords.

When shutting off the power, if you have time, it is best practice to:

1. First shut off individual breakers/fuses.
2. Then shut off the main breaker/fuse.

This will avoid a power surge which could happen by overloading the circuits when shutting off the main breaker. It can cause severe damage to appliances and even start a fire.

When turning the power back on:

3. First turn on the main switch/breaker,
4. Then turn on the individual breakers/fuses.

DO NOT enter a flooded area to shut off the electricity. After a natural disaster such as an earthquake or hurricane, keep the power off until a trained professional can inspect your home for potential gas leaks.

WATER

In case of a major disaster (earthquake, tsunami, mudslide) the water supply network might be damaged, and the water contaminated.

Shut off the water if:

- you notice a leak, or
- you experience low water pressure.

Label the water valve with a tag. If this valve can't be completely shut off (because of rust for example), replace it promptly.

Prioritizing personal safety ensures a more secure response to emergency situations. Regardless of the circumstances, do not take any unreasonable risks when shutting off your utilities.

HOME FIRE

In the event of a home fire, every second counts. It takes less than a minute for a small flame to ignite a fire that quickly spirals out of control and turns into a major blaze. Within minutes, a house can fill with thick black smoke and become engulfed in flames.

CLASSES OF FIRE

Fires are categorized into classes according to the type of fuel that is burning.

Class A fire: ordinary combustibles such as paper, cloth, wood, rubber, and many plastics.

Class B fire: flammable and combustible liquids (e.g., oils, gasoline, charcoal, lighter fluid, alcohol) burn only at the surface because oxygen cannot penetrate the depth of the fluid.

Class C fire: live electrical equipment (e.g., electric panel, oven, microwave, wiring, motors). When the electricity is turned off, the fire typically becomes a Class A fire.

Class D fire: combustible metals, such as sodium, magnesium, and titanium.

Class K fire: kitchen fires such as cooking oils or fats in cooking appliances. Note: Never use water to extinguish a Class K fire.

FIRE EXTINGUISHERS

Fires are categorized into classes according to the type of fuel that is burning.

Class A extinguishers use water or certain types of dry chemicals to either absorb heat or coat the fire.

Class B extinguishers will expel CO_2, remove the oxygen and suffocate the fire.

Class C extinguishers include CO_2 (like class B extinguisher), dry chemicals, clean agents (halon and/or halocarbon agents). Water-based extinguishers can be effective to put out a class C fire but are dangerous to use.
Note: the area will be dangerous until the power source is disconnected

Class D extinguishers use dry powder which will not react with the material. Common extinguishing agents may react with a combustible metal and increase the severity of the fire.

Multipurpose fire extinguishers with an ABC rating are suitable for use with fires involving ordinary combustibles, flammable liquids and energized electrical equipment as well as kitchen fires.

PUTTING OUT A SMALL FIRE AT HOME

 Remember that the top priority will always be able to get out safely.

1 Call 911.

2 Quickly assess the situation:

- Is there anyone injured?
- Do you have the right type of extinguisher?
- Check Your Extinguisher Functionality (the pressure gauge must be in the green area)?
- Are there any hazardous materials in the fire area (like flammable materials or falling debris)?
- Do you have at least two ways to exit the area?

3 Operate your fire extinguisher:

Pull the pin out and test the extinguisher.

Aim at the base of the fire.

Squeeze the handle.

Sweep side to side holding the hose.

4 Overhaul the fire to be sure that it is extinguished.

PUTTING OUT A SMALL FIRE AT HOME

- Keep your distance with the fire, the average range of dry chemical extinguishers is 8-12 feet.
- If the fire starts expanding, leave the building immediately.
- Stay low on the ground, keep your mouth and nose covered to avoid breathing smoke.
- When approaching a closed door, use the back of your hand to touch the doorknob and door surface, checking for any signs of fire on the other side.
- If either feels hot, don't open the door and use an alternative escape route.
- If the door feels cool, open it slowly, but be prepared to shut it promptly if you encounter heavy smoke or fire.
- Confine the fire by closing doors.
- If you are unable to exit, close the door and seal vents and cracks around doors to prevent smoke from entering. Stay in place and signal for help.
- Never turn your back on a fire.
- Meet at your designated meeting place outside
- Once out, do not go back in for any reason.

PREPARED

EMERGENCY PLAN

EMERGENCY PLAN BASICS

Preparing an emergency plan will give you peace of mind and more assurance in a crisis to keep calm and to do what you need to do.

You will know how to start, and it will significantly reduce the risk of freezing in times when action is required.

According to your personal assessment, develop your emergency plan, step by step.

Start by having a conversation with your loved ones and household members about:

- when to evacuate your home and when to shelter in place,
- where will you meet and how will you communicate if you're separated during an emergency.

Your emergency plan should answer the following questions:

WHAT   Identify and prepare for potential disasters specific to your area that may impact your home, workplace, and community.

WHY   Communicate, regroup, evacuate, shelter in place, provide first aid, protect, repair.

WHO   1st circle: family members, households. 2nd circle: neighbors, local community. Out-of-town contact: liaison contact.

WHEN   For large-scale disasters or crisis situations that disrupt daily life.

WHERE   Consider the places where you are most of the time: home, at work and commuting.

HOW   An elementary plan becomes very complicated in a crisis (the stress effect), so keep it simple.

WHAT IF You can't foresee everything, so prepare alternate solutions within your plan.

41

SHELTER IN PLACE

Sheltering is a safety measure to be taken when emergencies arise, requiring you to seek refuge in a secure location such as your home, workplace, or other designated area. The duration of sheltering varies depending on the specific emergency situation.

It is crucial to stay informed through reliable sources and follow the guidance and instructions provided by local authorities to ensure your safety.

If local authorities' information is not immediately available, use your best judgment and any available information to evaluate the situation and decide if there is an immediate threat to your safety. Trust your instincts and take necessary precautions to protect yourself and your family.

During prolonged sheltering periods, it's important to effectively manage your water and food supplies to ensure you and your family have sufficient resources to sustain yourselves for an extended time.

Sheltering can involve two possible options, depending on the circumstances: **remaining at home or seeking refuge in a designated safe room.**

SHELTERING IN YOUR SAFE ROOM

Identify and prepare a safe room in advance, considering its location within your home, ease of access, the number and type of doors it has, as well as minimal windows and external walls.

- Bring everyone inside and lock all doors and windows, don't forget your pets.
- Grab your family emergency kit.
- Stay informed by having multiple ways to receive alerts including a battery-powered or hand crank radio on hand, which will continue to provide vital information even if other forms of communication fail.
- If you have to create a barrier between you and potentially hazardous air outside:
  - Close air vents, fireplace dampers, and turn off fans, air conditioning, and heating systems.
  - Seal all openings with plastic sheeting and duct tape, preparing sheets in advance if possible. Start by taping the corners, then secure all edges.
  - Be resourceful and use available materials to create a barrier against potential contamination.
- Sheltering in place can be stressful, try to stay calm and patient. If you have kids, make sure they have toys, stuffed animals, or books that bring them comfort.
- Consider a portable charger for a tablet or handheld

console with their favorite games or shows. It's crucial to prioritize their emotional comfort and safety.

- Stay put in your safe room until officials say that it is safe to leave.

SHELTERING IN YOUR CAR

If you are driving, in certain emergency situations, it's safer to pull over and stay in your vehicle. If you can't get indoors quickly and safely:

- Pull over to the side of the road and stop your vehicle in a secure spot.
- Turn off the engine and stay put.
- Get your car emergency kit ready to be used.
- If it's warm outside, try to stop under a bridge or in a shaded area to avoid overheating.
- Keep listening to the radio for updates and additional instructions. Don't worry about draining your car battery; modern radios use minimal power, so you can listen for an hour or two without concern.
- Remain in your vehicle until authorities declare it safe to resume driving. Even after it's safe to get back on the road, continue listening to the radio and following law enforcement instructions.

MASS CARE SHELTER

While mass care shelters typically offer essential amenities like water, food, medicine, and basic sanitation facilities, it's crucial to bring your family emergency kit to ensure you have your own necessary supplies (soap, hand sanitizer, disinfecting wipes, …).

Additionally, be prepared for the challenges of communal living in close quarters with many people, which can be uncomfortable and stressful.

Note that while all shelters welcome service animals, many public shelters and hotels have pet-free policies, so it's essential to plan ahead and make arrangements for your pets if you need to evacuate.

During an emergency situation, **you can search for local open shelters by texting SHELTER and your ZIP code to 43362** (example: dial 43362 and text "Shelter 94016").

For more information, visit:
http://www.disasterassistance.gov/

EVACUATION CHECKLIST

Stay informed through updates from your local emergency management agencies. Sign up for local alert systems, such as Emergency Alert System (EAS), or other community-based notification systems. These can deliver critical information directly to your phone.

Evacuation warning

Evacuate as soon as possible. You might have a short delay to gather valuables or to prepare your home. Leave immediately if you feel unsafe or if conditions change.

Evacuation order

Evacuate immediately! Leave with no delay and follow any directions given by the authorities in the evacuation order. You won't have time to gather valuables or to prepare your home. Grab your emergency kit and leave.

Shelter in place may be required when evacuation is unnecessary, impossible or too dangerous. Stay at home or in your current location. Identify a safe room in your home and make a list of tasks and responsibilities for your household members.

EVACUATING YOUR HOME

- Check on your destination and your evacuation route before leaving.
- Have a primary evacuation route planned ahead as well as an alternate one.
- Stay informed and updated about the local situation.
- Follow the instructions of local officials.
- If you are driving, plug in your phone to keep it fully charged.
- Notify your out-of-area contact of your location, status and destination.
- If possible, gather your household members in one vehicle with adequate fuel.
- Drive slowly, be aware of your surroundings, turn on headlights.
- If possible, avoid tunnel and single lane bridges.
- If you have to leave your car, park it off the road. Notify your out-of-area contact.
- Upon arrival, notify your out-of-area contact.

EVACUATING YOUR HOME: TO DO

☐ Leave a note with your contact info and out-of-town contact on the fridge.

☐ Check on elderly or disabled neighbors.

☐ Dress all family members according to the weather conditions and type of emergency.

☐ If you are evacuating because of a fire:

☐ Long sleeves and long pants made of cotton or wool (no matter how hot it is).

☐ Goggles, leather gloves, N95 respirator.

☐ Tie long hair back (hair is flammable).

☐ Make sure each member of your family is wearing a reflective band and an emergency whistle.

☐ Close all doors and windows outdoor and indoor.

☐ Shut off ventilation, fans and air conditioning.

☐ Log out from every active account and shut off computers.

☐ Switch off all your electric breakers but the fridge and. freezer ones (make sure that all your breakers are clearly identified).

☐ ....

☐ ....

☐ ....

EVACUATING YOUR HOME: TO GRAB

- [ ] Family emergency kit
- [ ] Medications
- [ ] "Good to have" bag (extra clothing, shoes, food)
- [ ] Camping gear (sleeping bags)
- [ ] Food supplies (with a bag ready to pack) Water
- [ ] Toolbox
- [ ] Pet emergency bag with extra food
- [ ] Pet carrier (with pet inside)
- [ ] Cell phone chargers and cables
- [ ] House and cars keys
- [ ] Toiletry bag
- [ ] Important documents (folder)
- [ ] Personal photos
- [ ] Valuables
- [ ] Laptops
- [ ] Hard drives
- [ ] ....
- [ ] ....
- [ ] ....
- [ ] ....

ESSENTIAL DOCUMENTS

For quick accessibility and security, it is recommended scanning and saving your critical documents on a secure flash drive (encrypted and password-protected). Place the flash drive in a waterproof pouch for added protection and ease of locating, given its small size.

Additionally, consider storing an extra copy on a secure cloud platform for alternative access. As always, you should customize it according to your individual requirements.

PERSONALIZED EMERGENCY PLAN

☐ Emergency plan: personal guidelines, contact list, evacuation plan, communication strategy.

CONTACT INFORMATION

☐ People included in your emergency plan, including your out-of-town contact.

☐ Family members.

☐ Close relatives and friends.

☐ School and daycare providers.

☐ Professional contacts.

☐ Local police department, fire and emergency services (other than 911).

SAFE PREPARED EQUIPPED

FAMILY DOCUMENTS

- ☐ Birth certificates.
- ☐ Naturalization or citizenship documents.
- ☐ Social Security cards.
- ☐ Passports and driver's license.
- ☐ Marriage and divorce documents.
- ☐ Adoption and custody decrees.
- ☐ Military documents.
- ☐ Recent photographs of family.
- ☐ Degrees, professional licenses and certifications.
- ☐ Secured list of logins and passwords of your different accounts (social media, email…).

- ☐ ....
- ☐ ....
- ☐ ....
- ☐ ....

LEGAL AND FINANCIAL DOCUMENTS

☐ Tax and Income information - at least last year's tax returns.

☐ Personal and business property tax statements.

☐ Titles of all properties you own, real estate deeds.

☐ Financial account numbers, credit cards numbers and bank contact information.

☐ Retirement/pension statements.

☐ Employment records.

☐ All insurance policies documentation and contact information.

☐ Bills and loans information- going through a disaster does not mean you can stop paying your bills.

☐ Will and living will - a personal directive for medical decisions, such as life support, organ donation, name of the person who is allowed to make medical decisions if you are not able to do so for yourself.

☐ A legal document naming the person with the power to act on your behalf for financial or legal concerns if you are not able to do so for yourself (Power of Attorney).

☐ ....

MEDICAL DOCUMENTS AND INFORMATION

- ☐ Medical insurance information and contacts.
- ☐ Vaccination records.
- ☐ Allergy information.
- ☐ Medications list and prescriptions.
- ☐ Crucial medical records.
- ☐ Utility emergency numbers.
- ☐ ....
- ☐ ....

PETS' DOCUMENTS AND INFORMATION

- ☐ Pets microchip numbers.
- ☐ Medical insurance information and contacts.
- ☐ Vaccination records.
- ☐ Allergy information.
- ☐ Medications list and prescriptions.
- ☐ Recent photographs of pets - if you are separated and need to get help finding them.
- ☐ ....
- ☐ ....

DIGITAL COPY OF FAMILY KEEPSAKES

☐ Meaningful family photos, videos and memories.

☐ ....

☐ ....

VIDEO INSURANCE INVENTORY

☐ Record a walk-through video of your home to make an inventory of your belongings for insurance purposes (with brand names and serial numbers, eventually certificate for valuables).

COMMUNICATION PLAN

COMMUNICATION IS KEY

Your communication plan should be designed to address two scenarios:

1. You still have access to the mobile network.

2. You don't have any mobile network or Internet access.

- Include a list of alert systems available in your area in your communication plan, ensuring you know how to stay informed. Share this information with the individuals included in your emergency plan.
- In your plan, include a section with contact information for household members, including phone numbers, emails, and login details for other applications such as WhatsApp groups.
- Identify and include an out-of-town or out-of-town contact in your plan.
- Make a note of essential and emergency services in your vicinity, including medical contacts, schools, daycares, workplaces, and utilities.
- Ensure that everyone included in your emergency plan is familiar with and understands the details. It's also crucial to brief your out-of-town contact on the plan.
- Regularly review your emergency plan and test your devices to ensure you know how to use them, and that you have a way to charge them.

YOU STILL HAVE ACCESS TO
THE MOBILE NETWORK

- Make a communication plan specifying which device or application to use and the preferred mode of communication.
- Prioritize text messaging due to its lower bandwidth usage.
- In case the message cannot be delivered immediately, it will continue to attempt delivery, ensuring delayed but eventual transmission.
- You can use applications like WhatsApp to establish a dedicated group for emergency communication. Include your out-of-town contact in the group, enabling them to relay information as necessary.

YOU DON'T HAVE ANY MOBILE
NETWORK OR INTERNET ACCESS

- Each member of your family or household should know in advance what to do in such situations:
- How to return home and reconnect with family members.
- When, where, and how to evacuate with meeting places and predetermined routes.
- How to signal if help is needed.
- What protective actions to take to reduce risks based on the situation.

OUT-OF-TOWN CONTACT

Having an out-of-town contact in your emergency communication plan is crucial.

- Family members may be separated during an emergency, your out-of-town contact can serve as a central point of contact for everyone to check in and confirm their safety.
- Local phone lines and cell towers may be damaged or overwhelmed making it difficult to reach local contacts.
- Select an out-of-town contact who lives in a different city or even a different state and who is unlikely to be affected by the same emergency as you (at least 100 miles away from you).
- In cases of widespread evacuation, your out-of-town contact can provide updates about the situation.
- Knowing that there is a designated person to reach out can reduce panic and anxiety, as family members know who to contact to get updates and information.
- Your out-of-town contact can also act as a hub for information, relaying updates to other family members who may be outside the disaster zone.
- Your out-of-town contact must be aware of their role and responsibilities and is ideally someone who is known and trusted by your household members.
- Each family member should have your out-of-town contact information in their cell phone and printed on their personal information card.

PHONETIC ALPHABET

The international phonetic alphabet is a set of code words used for communicating the letters of the Roman alphabet for clear communication.

A - ALFA	N - NOVEMBER
B - BRAVO	O - OSCAR
C - CHARLIE	P - PAPA
D - DELTA	Q - QUEBEC
E - ECHO	R - ROMEO
F - FOXTROT	S - SIERRA
G - GOLF	T - TANGO
H - HOTEL	U - UNIFORM
I - INDIA	V - VICTOR
J - JULIETT	W - WHISKEY
K - KILO	X - XRAY
L - LIMA	Y - YANKEE
M - MIKE	Z - ZULU

Example:

"Emergency" will be communicated as follow:

Echo - Mike - Echo - Romeo - Golf - Echo - November - Charlie – Yankee

POWER OUTAGE

PREPARE FOR A POWER OUTAGE

- Make a list of the essential items you use every day that require electricity, this will help you identify what you need to prepare for.
- Consider stocking up on batteries and alternative power sources, like portable chargers or power banks (ensure that they're fully charged!).
- Each household member should have their own flashlight, readily accessible and in good working condition.
- Check whether your home phone is a cordless phone that requires electricity or a traditional landline phone that works during power outages. If it's cordless, find out how long the battery backup will last and plan accordingly.
- Be aware of medical needs or requirements in your household, specifically medical devices powered by electricity and refrigerated medicines.
- Consider keeping your vehicles' gas tanks at least half full, and have some cash reserved at home in small bills for emergency purchases.
- Have an AM/FM radio that can run on batteries, solar power, or hand crank. Remember to check and note the local frequency beforehand.
- Leave one light on so you know when power returns.

APPLIANCES DURING POWER OUTAGES

- Camp stoves, and grills should only be used outdoors and away from windows.
- Never use a gas stovetop or oven for home heating.
- Turn off or disconnect appliances and electronics during a power outage. This will prevent damage from power surges or spikes when power returns.

GENERATOR SAFETY

- Portable backup generators can produce carbon monoxide (CO), a deadly gas which is odorless and colorless.
- Always use generators outside, away from windows and doors.
- Never run a generator in a garage even if doors and
- windows are open.
- Keep generators at least 20 feet from your home and windows.
- Install CO detectors in your home and check batteries regularly.
- Symptoms of CO poisoning include headache, dizziness, nausea, and confusion.
- If you suspect CO poisoning, get outside immediately and call 911.

FOOD STORAGE

- Stock up on non-perishable food and water for at least one week per household member.
- During a power outage, keep freezers and refrigerators closed as much as possible. Refrigerators can typically keep food cold for 4 hours and full freezers for 2 days. Utilize coolers with ice if needed.
- Monitor temperatures with a thermometer and discard food if it reaches 40°F or higher.
- A full freezer can help keep the temperature consistent due to the density of frozen food and containers. Fill empty space in your freezer with containers of water to extend the temperature longevity during a power outage. This will also increase your water storage.
- The freezer coin tip: place a coin on top of an ice cube or of a glass of frozen water in your freezer before the power goes out. If the coin sinks into the ice, it means the freezer's temperature has risen above 32°F (0°C), indicating potential food spoilage.
- If you rely on well water, the pump requires electricity to function. So, before a heavy storm hits, make sure to stock up on drinking water.

- A fridge's normal temperature is 40° F (4° C), it will keep food safe for 4 hours.
- A freezer's normal temperature is 0° F (-18° C), it will hold its temperature for 48 hours, and for 24 hours if it is half full.
- You should throw out perishable food in your refrigerator (meat, fish, eggs, milk, and leftovers, cut fruits and vegetables) after 4 hours without power or a cold source.
- Throw out any food with an unusual odor, color, or texture.
- Never taste food to determine if it is safe to eat. When in doubt, throw it out.

EARTHQUAKE

MAGNITUDE SCALE

The Richter magnitude measures the amount of seismic energy released by an earthquake, with each whole number increase on the scale representing a tenfold increase in amplitude of the seismic waves and approximately 31.6 times more energy release.

Most seismological authorities use other comparable scales, such as the moment magnitude scale, but much of the news media still mistakenly refers to these as "Richter" magnitudes.

| Magnitude | Potential impacts
(depending on infrastructure preparedness) |
|:---:|---|
| 1 | Can only be detected by seismograph. |
| 2 | Smallest quake that people might feel. |
| 3 | Can be felt around the epicenter, hanging objects may swing. |
| 4 | May cause objects to fall and break windows. |
| 5 | Furniture might move or fall if not secured, damage to weak buildings. |
| 6 | Damage to well built structures, severe damage to weak ones. |
| 7 | Serious damage to structures including foundations, cracks in the earth. |
| 8 | Major destruction to structures, bridges collapsed. |
| 9 | Extreme destruction, most structures destroyed or severely damaged. |

PREPARE FOR AN EARTHQUAKE

- Secure heavy items (furniture, television, water heater, …) and hanging objects in your home.
- Secure or remove objects that could block doorways.
- Move beds away from windows.
- Keep a flashlight and shoes under the beds.
- Make an emergency plan for reuniting family members.
- Develop a communication plan, including an out-of-town contact.
- Build a customized emergency kit.
- Practice drop, cover and hold on.

STAY SAFE DURING AN EARTHQUAKE

- In any situation: protect your head, neck and eyes.
- Drop down, cover your head and neck and hold on to something sturdy.
- Protect against falling objects.
- Stay away from glass and windows.
- Get beneath a table, bench or desk.
- Don't run outside.
- If you are outdoors: stay away from buildings and falling wires.
- If you are driving: pull off the road and park in the open, stay in your car until the tremors are over.

STAY SAFE AFTER AN EARTHQUAKE

- Check if yourself or others are injured.
- Protect your mouth, nose and eyes from dust.
- Watch for debris and things that might fall.
- If you are trapped, bang on a wall, a sturdy surface or a pipe, if you have a whistle, use it rather than shouting.
- Use text messages or social media to communicate.
- Check for leaking gas, if you smell gas, open the windows,
- get out of the house and call 911 or the gas company.
- If you are in an area at risk of tsunamis, go to higher
- ground.
- Expect aftershocks.
- Listen to local news and emergency instructions.

SECONDARY IMPACTS OF EARTHQUAKES

Tsunamis may happen as a result of the displacement of substantial water volumes caused by fault slippage beneath the ocean if earthquakes occur in the sea.

Liquefaction is a phenomenon that occurs when saturated soils lose strength due to strong ground shaking.

Landslides can be triggered by earthquakes in mountainous or hilly regions, where stresses can cause weak slopes to fail.

Fires, building collapse, dam failure are also potential secondary hazards following an earthquake.

WILDFIRE

PREPARE FOR A WILDFIRE

- Sign up for local emergency warnings and alerts. During a wildfire, the most important information will come from your local government.
- Clear area of leaves & other combustible debris at least 30 ft around your home.
- Have an outdoor water source with a hose long enough to reach any area of your property.
- Have an evacuation plan, know your routes (at least 2 different ones) and destinations.
- Check your emergency kits: at least 3 days of supplies in case of evacuation, 1 week in case of shelter in place.
- Anticipate a power outage (flashlight and batteries).
- Inform your out-of-town contact about your situation (do this when you still have a mobile network).

STAY SAFE DURING A WILDFIRE

- Evacuate immediately if authorities tell you to do so!
- If you feel you are in danger don't wait for an official notice to evacuate.
- If you have to evacuate, wear appropriate clothing to protect your skin and hair (goggles, face-mask, long-sleeved shirts, long pants, shoes and socks, hat).
- If driving, close windows and vents, drive slowly with headlights on.
- If ordered to by local authorities, follow evacuation routes and do not try to take shortcuts.
- If you stay home, close every window, door and vent.
- If trapped, fill sinks and tubs with water, turn on lights to be more visible and call 911.
- Stay away from outside walls and windows.
- Use a face-mask to protect from smoke and particles.

STAY SAFE AFTER A WILDFIRE

- If you had to evacuate, return home only if local authorities say it is safe.
- Inspect your home damages with caution.
- Remaining burning embers may reignite and the ground may contain heat pockets.
- Be aware of hot ash, charred trees, and smoldering debris.
- Wear protective clothing to clean-up, long-sleeved shirts, long pants, closed shoes and socks, work gloves, face-mask, goggles.
- Avoid direct contact with ash.
- Douse debris and extinguish burning embers to reduce smoke and dust.
- Quickly rinse away any ash that comes into contact with your skin, eyes, or mouth.
- Individuals with asthma, heart issues, lung conditions, pregnant women, and children should avoid inhaling ash dust.

SMOKE SAFETY

SMOKE IMPACTS ON HEALTH

- Depending on length of exposure and concentration of particulate matter.
- Eye irritation: smoke particles can cause irritation to the eyes, resulting in redness, itching, and tearing.
- Respiratory issues: inhaling smoke can irritate the respiratory system, leading to coughing, wheezing, shortness of breath, and chest discomfort.
- Aggravation of pre-existing conditions: smoke can exacerbate pre-existing respiratory conditions such as asthma, chronic bronchitis, or other lung diseases.
- Increased risk for vulnerable populations: children, older adults, and individuals with pre-existing health conditions.
- Long-term health impacts: prolonged exposure to high levels of smoke may contribute to chronic respiratory conditions and increase the risk of cardiovascular issues over time.

PROTECT AND REDUCE EXPOSURE OUTDOOR

- Monitor air quality, check local agency's website or www.airnow.gov
- Reduce physical activities.
- While driving: close windows and vents, run air conditioning in recirculate mode.
- Slow down if you drive in smoky conditions.
- Don't rely on dust masks or bandanas for smoke protection, a N95 respirator can protect you more effectively, provided it fits snugly on your face and is worn correctly.

THE U.S. AIR QUALITY INDEX

The U.S. Air Quality Index (AQI) is the Environmental Protection Agency's (EPA) method for communicating daily air quality information. Go on https://www.airnow.gov/ or download the EPA AirNow application.

Air Quality Index scale	
0 - 50	Good
51 - 100	Moderate
101 - 150	Unhealthy for sensitive groups
151 - 200	Unhealthy
201 - 300	Very unhealthy
301 - 500	Hazardous
+500	Beyond AQI scale

PROTECT AND REDUCE EXPOSURE INDOOR

- Monitor air quality, check local agency's website or www.airnow.gov
- Stay inside with the doors, windows and vents closed.
- If you don't have an air conditioner and the temperature indoors is too high to remain with closed windows, consider seeking shelter elsewhere.
- Face-mask: N95 respirator provides the best protection if it fits snugly to your face.
- Create a "clean room" with no fireplace and as few windows and doors as possible; use a portable air cleaner sized for the room and that doesn't make ozone (air pollutant).
- Reduce indoor pollution: don't use candles, burning stoves, tobacco, aerosol, fry & broil cooking, vacuum.
- Air out your home when it is safe to do so.

HEAT WAVE

HEAT RELATED ALERTS FROM THE NATIONAL WEATHER SERVICE

Excessive Heat Watches

Issued when the risk of a heat wave has increased but its occurrence and timing (in the next 24 to 72 hours) is still uncertain.

Heat Advisory

Issued within 12 hours of the onset of extreme heat conditions: maximum heat index temperature expected to be 100°F (37,7°C) or higher for at least 2 days, and nighttime air temperatures will not drop below 75° F (24°C).

Excessive Heat Warning

Issued within 12 hours of the onset of extreme heat conditions: maximum heat index temperature expected to be 105°F (40.5°C) or higher for at least 2 days and nighttime air temperatures will not drop below 75°F (24°C).

Note: temperature criteria vary across the country, especially for areas not used to extreme heat conditions.

Heat index is the temperature the body feels when the effects of heat and humidity are combined.

72

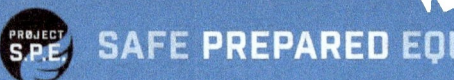
BE PREPARED FOR A HEAT WAVE

- Be informed, listen to local weather forecasts, and stay aware of upcoming heat alerts.
- Plan your activities accordingly (home, work, sports, outdoor).
- Identify places you could go during the warmest hours (libraries, theaters, malls, other places with air conditioning).
- People living in urban areas may be at greater risk from the effects of a prolonged heat wave.
- Learn what to do in case of a heat related illness.
- Ensure that you have enough water at your disposal.
- Check on those in your neighborhood who are more vulnerable to heat.

BE SAFE DURING A HEAT WAVE

- If you're outside, find shade, protect your head with a hat.
- Dress in lightweight, loose-fitting, light-colored clothing.
- If you're inside, prefer north facing rooms, draw window blinds, use space blankets to keep the heat out (check the space blanket flash card).
- Drink plenty of fluids: **don't wait until you are thirsty!**
- Avoid alcohol and caffeine.
- Eat light meals (digestion slightly increases the body temperature).
- Use cool compresses, showers, and baths.
- Avoid high-energy activities. If you are working, take breaks frequently (specifically for outdoor workers).
- Never leave children or pets inside a vehicle on a warm day.
- Check on your neighbors to ensure that they are not suffering from the heat.
- If you have pets: ensure they always have water at their disposal.

   Check the Heat related illness flashcard.

   In any case, if you are uncertain about the signs of heat related illness or about what to do, call 911.

74

HURRICANE

THE SAFFIR-SIMPSON
HURRICANE SCALE

The Saffir-Simpson Hurricane Wind Scale is a classification system used to categorize hurricanes based on their maximum sustained wind speeds.

Cat 1 74 to 95 mph (119 to 153 km/h): very dangerous winds - structural damages, mostly roof, some trees down, local power outages, minimal coastal flooding.

Cat 2 96 to 110 mph (154 to 177 km/h): extremely dangerous winds - roof and other major damages, roads blocked, whole area power outages.

Cat3 111 to 129 mph (178 to 208 km/h): devastating winds - roofs ripped off and other major damages, uprooted trees, weeks long power outages.

Cat 4 130 to 156 mph (209 to 251 km/h): catastrophic winds - severe damage to well-built structures, most trees uprooted, weeks long power outages.

Cat 5 157 mph (252 km/h) or higher: catastrophic winds - destruction of most framed structures, most trees uprooted, most of the area could be uninhabitable for weeks or months.

75

BE PREPARED FOR A HURRICANE

- Stay informed: listen to local alert systems, and NOAA Weather Radio.
- Protect doors and windows.
- Store lawn furniture, gardening tools, trash cans (away from home exits).
- Clear gutters and drains to prevent flooding.
- Have an evacuation plan, know your routes and destinations.
- Check your emergency kit.
- Anticipate a power outage (flashlight and batteries). Inform your out-of-town contact about your situation (do it when you still have a mobile network).
- Be prepared to live without power, water, gas, phone, and Internet for many days.
- Follow evacuation routes and do not try to take shortcuts.

BE SAFE DURING A HURRICANE

- Stay indoors, in a designated room (away from windows).
- Avoid floodwater (it may carry debris and be contaminated).
- If you are trapped by flooding, go to the highest level but **never go in a closed attic, without windows or access to the roof.**
- Stay informed: listen to local alerting systems, and NOAA Weather Radio.

STAY SAFE AFTER A HURRICANE

- Prefer text messages or social media to communicate.
- If you had to evacuate, return home only if local authorities say it is safe.
- Don't drive unless there is an emergency.
- Stay away from loose or fallen power lines.
- Inspect your home structure with caution.
- Wear work gloves and boots during clean up, use face-masks if mold can be seen or smelled.
- People with health conditions (especially asthma and lung conditions) should avoid buildings where mold can be seen or smelled.
- Avoid wading in flood water, which will probably contain debris and be contaminated.
- Be aware that snakes and other animals may have gotten into flooded buildings.
- Do not touch electrical equipment if you are standing in water.
- Turn off the electricity if it is safe to do so.

FLOOD

**NATIONAL WEATHER SERVICE
MESSAGING TERMINOLOGY**

Flood Watch: issued when conditions are favorable for flooding, indicating that flooding is possible but not yet certain. It serves as a heads-up to alert individuals to be prepared and monitor the situation closely.

→ **Be Prepared.**

Flood Advisory: issued when a specific weather event is forecasted to cause minor flooding or nuisance conditions but is not expected to be severe enough to warrant a warning.

→ **Be Aware.**

Flood Warning: is issued when a hazardous flood, is imminent or already occurring. It's the highest level of alert, indicating a dangerous situation that requires immediate action to protect oneself and property.

→ **Take Action.**

Flash Flood Warning: issued when a flash flood is imminent or already happening. A flash flood is a sudden and violent flood that can develop in a matter of minutes to hours, and it's possible to experience one even in areas not receiving rain directly. Move immediately to higher ground.

→ **Take Action.**

BE PREPARED FOR A FLOOD

- Stay informed: listen to local alerting systems, and NOAA Weather Radio.
- Have an evacuation plan, know your routes and destinations.
- Check your emergency kit.
- Anticipate a power outage (flashlight and batteries).
- Inform your out-of-town contact about your situation (do it when you still have a mobile network).
- Be prepared to live without power, water, gas, phone, and Internet for many days.
- Stay off bridges over fast-moving water.
- Stay away from beaches and rivers banks.
- Stay away from areas that could potentially be flooded (basement, underpasses, underground metro station).
- Depending on the type of flood warning: move to higher ground or a higher floor, evacuate if told to do so.
- Inform your out-of-town contact about your situation (do it when you still have a mobile network).
- Obey evacuation orders immediately, follow evacuation routes and do not try to take shortcuts.

BE SAFE DURING A FLOOD

- Don't walk or swim through flood waters: six inches of fast-moving water can knock you down.
- Don't drive through flood waters: one foot of fast-moving water can sweep your vehicle away.
- If caught with your car on a flooded road with rising waters, get out and move quickly to higher ground.
- Follow local emergency responders' instructions.
- Stay off bridges over fast-moving water.
- Stay away from the banks of rivers, streams, and creeks.
- If trapped in a building, get to the highest level but never get into a closed attic without windows or access to the roof.
- If you use tap water, boil it until water sources have been declared safe (check SAFE - Water treatment's flashcard).

STAY SAFE AFTER A FLOOD

- If you had to evacuate, return home only if local authorities say it is safe.
- Don't drive unless there is an emergency.
- Stay away from loose or fallen power lines.
- Wear work gloves and boots during clean up.
- Use face-masks if mold can be seen or smelled.
- Dispose of any food, drinks and medication that got in contact with flood water.
- People with health conditions (especially asthma and lung conditions) should avoid buildings where mold can be seen or smelled.
- Keep children and pets away from floodwater.
- Avoid wading in flood water, which will probably contain debris and be contaminated.
- Be aware that snakes, other animals and insects may have gotten into flooded buildings.
- Do not touch electrical equipment if you are standing in water, don't use appliances that have been flooded.
- Turn off the electricity if it is safe to do so.

TORNADO

A tornado is a vertical rotating column of air created during violent thunderstorms called supercells.

Supercells contain a strong rotating updraft and can produce severe weather, including damaging winds, heavy rainfall, large hail, and ultimately tornadoes.

TORNADO ALERTS

In the US, tornado watches and warnings are issued by the National Oceanic and Atmospheric Administration (NOAA) Storm Prediction Center which watches the weather 24/7 across the entire country.

Tornado watch: the weather conditions are favorable for tornadoes and severe weather. A watch usually covers many counties or even states.

→ **You need to get ready:** check on the people around you, check your supplies, your emergency kits and your safe room.

Tornado warning: a tornado has been reported indicated by weather radar. A warning typically covers a smaller area, like a city or small county. There is imminent danger to life and property. **According to the NOAA, the average lead-time for tornado warnings is 13 minutes.**

→ **You need to take action immediately**, take your emergency kits and move to your safe room.

82

TORNADO STRENGTH SCALE

Tornado strength is rated according to the Enhanced Fujita (EF) scale. The rating is determined by wind speed and by the damage caused (28 damage indicators such as building type, structures and trees).

Enhanced Fujita Scale		
Strength	Wind speed	Damages
EF0	65-85 mph (105-137 km/h)	**Light damage** to roofs and chimneys. Trees have large branches broken off.
EF1	86-110 mph (138-177 km/h)	**Moderate damage** to permanent structures' roofs. Winds can be severely stripped roofs, overturn mobile homes, shatter windows.
EF2	111-135 mph (178-217 km/h)	**Considerable damage** to permanent structures, including roof loss, mobile homes are destroyed. Vehicles can be lifted off the ground.
EF3	136-165 mph (218-266 km/h)	**Severe damage** to well-built structures. Unanchored homes are swept away. Vehicles are lifted off the ground. Wooded areas sustain extensive vegetation loss.
EF4	166-200 mph (267-322 km/h)	**Devastating damage** Well-built homes are reduced to a short pile of medium-sized debris on the foundation. Heavy vehicles can be picked up and thrown. Large, healthy trees are entirely debarked.
EF5	+200 mph (+322 km/h)	**Incredible damage** to well-built homes which can be taken off their foundations. Significant damage to high-rise buildings. Low-lying vegetation is shredded from the ground. Trees are debarked and snapped.

PREPARE FOR A TORNADO

- Sign up for email and text message alerts from your local emergency management office and make sure your mobile devices are set to receive wireless emergency alerts.
- If your community uses sirens, then become familiar with the warning tone.
- Stay informed about weather forecasts, as meteorologists can predict when conditions are likely to lead to tornadoes.
- Be aware of the signs of a tornado or supercell, such as a rotating, funnel-shaped cloud or a loud roar like a freight train.
- Identify a safe room designed to withstand high winds or find a small room with no windows on the lowest level of a sturdy building for the next best protection.
- During high wind events, mobile homes, manufactured homes, trailer homes, and recreational vehicles are not safe.
- Practice evacuating with your entire household to the safe locations you've identified. Remember, the average lead-time for a tornado warning is 13 minutes.

STAY SAFE DURING A TORNADO

- In case of a tornado warning alert, immediately go to your safe room.
- Don't wait for an official alert to take shelter if you feel you are in danger.
- Protect yourself by using your arms to cover your head and neck, you can also wear bike or skateboard helmets if you have any, use blankets to surround and protect you.
- If you are in your car, seek shelter in a sturdy building, if you can't, choose a low-lying area, such as a ditch or depression, and cover your head and neck with your arms.
- It's not a good idea to go under bridges as they can create a wind tunnel effect, increasing the danger from high winds and debris.

STAY SAFE AFTER A TORNADO

- Listen to local alerts and authorities for updated information.
- Stay clear of fallen power lines or broken utility lines.
- During clean-up, wear sturdy shoes, long pants, and work gloves to protect yourself from rough surfaces and sharp debris.
- Prefer text messages or social media to communicate with family and friends rather than phone calls.

TSUNAMI

A tsunami is characterized by a series of massive waves, caused most of the time by earthquakes, underwater landslides, volcanic eruptions.

A tsunami typically gets bigger as it approaches shore. This is because the ocean's depth decreases as it approaches land, causing the waves to compress and increase in height. This phenomenon is known as "shoaling." Additionally, the shape of the coastline and underwater topography can also contribute to the wave's amplification.

TSUNAMI ALERTS

Tsunami Information Statement: an earthquake has occurred, but there is no immediate threat of tsunami.

→ **Monitor local emergency information.**

Tsunami Watch: an earthquake has occurred in a distant location, a tsunami is considered possible.

→ **Monitor local emergency information, be prepared to take action.**

Tsunami Advisory: A tsunami with life-threatening waves is expected to hit or is already affecting the area.

→ **Stay out of the water and away from beaches and waterways. Monitor and follow instructions from local officials.**

Tsunami Warning: A tsunami that may cause dangerous coastal flooding accompanied by powerful currents is expected or occurring and may continue for several hours after initial arrival.

→ **Take immediate action! Move to high ground or inland, away from the water.**

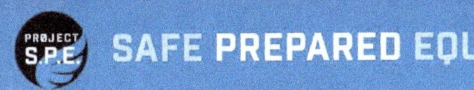

PREPARE FOR A TSUNAMI

- Find out if your home, school, workplace are in a tsunami hazard zone.
- Sign up for local emergency services alerts, make sure your mobile can receive wireless emergency alerts.
- Learn about your community's tsunami evacuation plan.
- Identify a safe place at least 100 feet (30 meters) above sea level or at least 1 mile (1.6 km) inland, away from waterways.
- Some reinforced concrete structures that are tall enough may offer a safe haven in their upper stories. However, this should only be considered as a last resort when all other evacuation options are unavailable.
- Practice walking your escape routes, including during nighttime and adverse weather conditions. This will help you become intimately familiar with the routes, making it easier and faster to evacuate in case of a real emergency.
- If your children attend school in an area prone to tsunamis, learn about the school's emergency protocols and procedures. Know where the designated assembly point is and where to retrieve your children once the danger has subsided.

STAY SAFE DURING A TSUNAMI

- Depending on your location, an official tsunami warning will be broadcast through local media, marine radio, wireless emergency alerts, text message or outdoor sirens.
- In case of natural signs of a potential tsunami, don't wait for an official alert, move quickly to higher ground or as far inland as possible.
- Natural signs of a potential tsunami include an earthquake, a loud roar from the ocean, an unusual ocean behavior, such as a sudden retreat or rise of the water.
- If you are outside of the tsunami hazard zone, stay where you are unless local authorities tell you otherwise.
- If you are caught in the water, grab onto anything that floats.
- If you are on a boat in a harbor, you should leave your boat and move quickly to a safe place on land.
- If you are on a boat at sea, you should move to a safe depth (depending on the region and the specific tsunami hazard, but the minimum safe depth is 180 feet or 55 meters) and stay away from harbors under warning until officials broadcast the end of the threat.
- Beware of receding water which can be as destructive as the initial tsunami waves.

STAY SAFE AFTER A TSUNAMI

- Stay out of the evacuation zone until local officials tell you it is safe.
- Listen to local alerts and authorities for information on areas to avoid.
- Prefer text messages or social media to communicate with family and friends rather than phone calls.
- Stay away from areas that have been damaged.
- Avoid roads and bridges that were flooded, they may be severely damaged and could collapse.
- Stay out of floodwater, which can conceal hazardous debris. Water may also be deeper than you think.
- Avoid fallen power lines or broken utility lines, avoid touching wet electrical equipment or standing in water.
- Stay informed about your local drinking water safety,
- Tsunamis can contaminate water supplies.

AVALANCHE

An avalanche is a mass of snow, ice, and rocks which slides quickly down a mountainside.

Snow avalanches most commonly occur within 24 hours of new snowfall, especially if more than 30 centimeters (12 inches) has accumulated on 30 to 45-degree slopes.

Avalanches can reach speeds of 80 mph within 5 seconds; the largest ones can even travel up to 200 mph (320 kmh). While falling off a mountainside, the mass and speed of the snow pressurize the air below it, producing a powerful and destructive wind capable of blowing a house apart (large avalanches).

The North American Public Avalanche Danger Scale (NAPADS) rates avalanche danger, providing travel advice based on likelihood, size, and distribution of expected avalanches across three elevation bands. Note: danger increases exponentially with each level.

1 - Low: generally safe avalanche conditions.

2 - Moderate: heightened avalanche conditions on specific terrain features.

3 - Considerable: dangerous avalanche conditions.

4 - High: Very dangerous avalanche conditions.

5 - Extreme: extraordinary dangerous avalanche conditions.

BE PREPARED FOR AN AVALANCHE

- Understand the risk of avalanches in your surroundings:
- Sign up for alerts from the U.S. Forest Service Avalanche Center and local alert systems.
- Follow avalanche warnings on roads.
- Know the signs of increased danger, including recent avalanches and visible cracks on fresh snow.
- Avoid increased risk areas, such as slopes steeper than 30 degrees.
- When hiking, skiing or doing any other activity in a risk area, make sure not to travel alone.
- Before departing, share your itinerary with someone who can communicate it to rescue teams in the event that you become trapped in an avalanche.
- Get proper equipment to keep yourself safe and alert rescuers:
  - Wear a helmet to reduce head injuries and create air pockets.
  - Wear an avalanche airbag, an inflatable system deployed out of a backpack, that may help you from being completely buried (the human body is three times denser than avalanche debris and will sink quickly).
  - Carry an avalanche beacon to help rescuers locate you.
  - Carry a first aid kit adapted to cold weather conditions.
  - Carry a whistle, its blast is much louder than a

human scream, using it will also save your voice, your energy and your body heat.
- ○ Carry a foldable shovel to help rescue others.

BE SAFE DURING AN AVALANCHE

- Try to make your way to one side of the avalanche.
- The ultimate goal is to get away using swimming motions before the snow settles, when it does you will have little or no ability to move.
- If you can't, create as much breathing space, an "air pocket", in the snow as possible to prolong survival.

STAY SAFE AFTER AN AVALANCHE

- If you can, immediately call 911.
- After an avalanche, the snow compacts and quickly becomes as solid as concrete and trapped victims are unable to dig out. People caught in avalanches can die from suffocation (75%), trauma or hypothermia. Survival rates drop dramatically in a short period of time for fully buried victims. An avalanche victim has a 93% survival rate if rescued within 15 minutes, it drops to 20% after 45 minutes of being buried, and after 2 hours, survival is rare.
- While survival is dependent on quick rescue, it might take some time for search and rescue crews to access the affected area. Therefore, successful rescue frequently depends on the closest responders possible, like the victim companions.

LANDSLIDE

BE AWARE OF LANDSLIDE RISKS

Topography and precipitation play crucial roles in landslide forecasting.

However, it is essential to also pay attention to the following factors:

- Landslides generally happen in areas where they have occurred in the past (steep slopes, canyons, riverbeds, channels).
- Heavily saturated ground is susceptible to mudflows and debris flows especially in areas with steep slopes.
- Multiple debris flows intensify the severity of a landslide by funneling into combined channels.
- Landslides are one of those disasters that can occur without warning, they can occur very quickly, with little or no notice, and some can move slowly, stopping for a bit and starting again.
- If you are near a wildfire burn area, pay attention to forecasts of rainfall.
- An increasingly rumbling sound, rushing water, trees cracking or boulders knocking together, might indicate moving debris.
- If you are near a creek or any other stream and notice a sudden increase or decrease in water flow or that water changes from clear to muddy, it could signal that there is debris flow activity upstream and that a landslide is coming.

94

BE PREPARED FOR A LANDSLIDE

- Pre-emptive evacuation is often the most effective measure to ensure the safety of yourself and your family in the face of a potential landslide.
- Stay informed about weather forecasts, geological assessments, and any official warnings issued by local authorities.
- Sign up for your community's warning system.
- Have an emergency kit readily available for a quick departure.
- Have an evacuation plan, make sure you and your family know what to do and where to go. Check that your evacuation route doesn't go through an area at risk of landslides (if known).
- Leave immediately if you have been told to by local authorities or if you feel it is unsafe to stay in your home.
- If there are signs of imminent danger, evacuate early to avoid potential road closures, traffic congestion, or other complications.
- You can't stop or change the path of a landslide, but you may be able to protect your property from minor floodwaters or mud by use of sandbags, retaining walls or by building channels. However, make sure you don't divert a flow to someone else's property.
- Check on neighbors, especially those who may need assistance, and encourage them to evacuate as well if needed.

BE SAFE DURING A LANDSLIDE

- By the time you know a debris flow is coming, your options will be limited, go to higher ground immediately.
- Never cross a road with water or mud flowing, the flow will increase suddenly in case of a landslide. Remember: six inches of fast-moving water can knock you down, one foot of fast-moving water can sweep your vehicle away.
- Never cross a bridge if you see a flow approaching as it can grow much faster and larger than you expect.
- If you do get stuck in the path of a landslide, move uphill as quickly as possible.
- Stay away from river valleys and any low-lying areas.

STAY SAFE AFTER A LANDSLIDE

- Ensure personal safety: stay away from the affected area, more debris could keep flowing after the main landslide.
- Evaluate the situation: examine your environment for imminent hazards, such as unstable slopes or continuous movement. Be vigilant for signs of additional landslides, including unusual sounds or ground movement.
- Be aware that flooding can follow a landslide, especially when it is due to excessive rainfall.
- Address any injuries and seek medical assistance for yourself and others if necessary. Use extra caution when assisting others and refrain from entering areas that are unstable or hazardous.
- Contact local emergency services to report the landslide.
- Provide information about the time, location, size, and any potential hazards.
- Check and report damages: home foundations, unstable infrastructures, utilities lines. Pictures of the affected area before and after the landslide will be helpful for damage assessment.
- Secure utilities: turn off utilities (gas, water, electricity) if there is damage to your home or the infrastructure.
- Remember: don't turn back on the gas yourself, call a qualified professional to do it.

VOLCANO ERUPTION

A volcano is a natural opening in the Earth's surface that enables the release of molten rock, gasses, and debris from beneath the crust.

Volcanic eruptions can unleash destructive forces and can be accompanied by a wide range of additional natural hazards, including lava flows, gas, pyroclastic flows, earthquakes, flash floods, lahar, rock falls and landslides, acid rain, fire, tsunamis, and more.

There are two main categories of volcanic eruptions:

Explosive eruptions, characterized by widespread ashfall, the release of hazardous hot gasses, volcanic rocks, and mudflows.

Quiet eruptions, marked by lava flows that can ignite fires and generate harmful gas clouds.

Volcanic eruptions often follow a cyclical pattern of increasing activity, providing some warning signs before an eruption occurs. However, the timeframe between the initial indications of volcanic unrest and the actual eruption can be relatively brief, ranging from a few days to several weeks or even months.

BE PREPARED FOR VOLCANO ERUPTION

- Know if you are in an area at risk and sign up for local government emergency alerts: the Volcano Notification Service (VNS) is a free service that sends you notification emails about volcanic activity happening at US monitored volcanoes.
- Have a shelter-in-place plan if your biggest risk is from ash.
- Have a shelter-in-place kit with essential supplies, and also be prepared to evacuate with a grab-and-go emergency kit.
- Plan to reconnect with loved ones if you are separated, have a communication plan including an out-of-town contact.
- Have an evacuation plan: know where you will go, how will you go, know your route and where you will stay.

BE SAFE DURING VOLCANO ERUPTION

- Listen for emergency information and alerts.
- Follow evacuation or shelter orders. If you have to evacuate, do it as early as possible.
- Keep away from areas downwind and river valleys downstream of the volcano, as they are vulnerable to the dangerous transport of debris and ash via wind and gravity.

Minimize your exposure to ash by taking these precautions:

- Limit outdoor activities and use a facemask if you must be outside.
- Protect yourself to prevent skin irritation, respiratory issues, eye problems, and infection in open wounds.
- Avoid areas downwind and river valleys downstream of the volcano.
- Seek temporary shelter in your current location, seal doors, windows, and ventilation openings to prevent ash entry.
- Avoid driving in heavy ash, but if you have to, keep windows closed and avoid using the air conditioning system.
- Refrain from attempting to remove ash from your roof.
- Stay indoors until authorities declare it safe to venture outside.

100

STAY SAFE AFTER VOLCANO ERUPTION

- Wait for official clearance from authorities before returning to your area after an eruption.
- Remain indoors until authorities declare it safe to venture outside.
- Refrain from driving in thick ashfall as it can: stir up ash, reducing visibility and creating hazardous conditions, clog engines and cause mechanical failure, stall vehicles, leaving you stranded.
- Avoid contact with ash if you have any breathing issues.
- Wear protective clothing and a facemask when cleaning up. Keep children safe and away from cleanup activities.
- Avoid attempting to remove ash from your roof unless you have received proper guidance. If you do, be aware that it can make surfaces slippery, and be mindful of your roof's weight capacity and avoid adding additional weight.
- Volcanic ash can contaminate drinking water sources, making them unsafe for consumption. Check with your local health department for updates on water safety and quality.
- Throw out food and beverages exposed to ash or smoke.

SOLAR STORM

Solar flares and Coronal Mass Ejections (CMEs) are the two primary components of a solar storm.

A solar flare is a burst of radiation containing a vast amount of energy, while a CME is a massive explosion of magnetized plasma off the sun's surface. While they can occur separately, when large ones occur together, it signals the start of a significant solar storm.

In these conditions, a solar flare is like the initial burst, while a CME is the powerful, lingering impact which can take many hours to several days to reach Earth, expanding in volume along the way. When it hits, the CME induces excess electricity in our planet's magnetosphere, triggering a geomagnetic storm, the most impactful aspect of a space-weather event.

Radiation from a solar flare can reach us in just over 8 minutes, which is the time it takes for light to travel the approximately 93 million miles between Earth and the sun.

Space weather experts can't really predict events in outer space. Instead, they focus on monitoring and understanding current space weather conditions to mitigate potential impacts on Earth as quickly as possible.

BE PREPARED FOR A SOLAR STORM'S IMPACTS

Solar storms can be unpredictable and challenging to communicate to the public in a timely manner. Therefore, the best way to prepare for their potential impacts is to prioritize global readiness and proactive measures to minimize disruptions and ensure resilience.

Direct potential impacts include power blackouts, loss of communications systems, disruption of satellite networks and GPS services, and utilities disruption.

- Be aware of your reliance on electricity and communications to anticipate disruptions in your daily life.
- Learn how to prepare for power outages.
- Make an emergency plan and a communication plan that can be implemented when Internet and mobile networks are down.
- Stay informed: Keep up to date with the latest solar weather forecasts and alerts from trusted sources.
- Unplug sensitive electronics and consider using surge protectors.

PANDEMIC

A pandemic is a disease outbreak that transcends national borders, impacting a significant portion of the global population.

Pandemics are most often caused by highly contagious viruses, which can transmit from one individual to another, facilitating rapid spread and widespread infection.

A pandemic differs from an epidemic which is a sudden increase in the number of cases of a disease but is typically contained within a limited region.

BE PREPARED FOR A PANDEMIC

Understanding how diseases are transmitted is crucial for safeguarding your health and the well-being of those around you. Viruses can spread through various means, including:

- Direct contact between individuals
- Indirect contact with contaminated objects or surfaces
- Asymptomatic carriers, who can unknowingly transmit the virus despite showing no symptoms themselves
- Review your health insurance policies to understand what's covered, including telemedicine services.
- Plan ahead for potential closures by setting up virtual options for school, work, and social activities, ensuring continuity and connection.
- Prepare for potential home confinement by stockpiling essentials like cleaning supplies, non-perishable food, prescriptions, and bottled water.

Remember: buy what you need, not what you can!

STAY SAFE DURING A PANDEMIC

- It's crucial to rely on official health organizations for accurate information and exercise caution when encountering rumors circulating on social media.
- Check your local and state public health departments for the most recent information on the disease, eventually on testing and vaccines. Stay up-to-date with the latest guidelines from the Centers for Disease Control and Prevention (CDC).
- Take these simple steps to prevent the spread of most contagious diseases:
    o Cover your mouth and nose when coughing or sneezing.
    o Regularly disinfect high-touch surfaces.
    o Wash your hands frequently with soap and water.
    o If soap and water are unavailable, use a hand sanitize with at least 60% alcohol.
    o Wear a mask in public areas.
    o Maintain a safe distance from individuals outside your household
    o Stay home if you're feeling unwell, unless seeking medical attention.
- During an epidemic or pandemic, it's common to feel anxious or stressed, especially when isolated. Remember, these feelings are normal. Don't hesitate to reach out and talk with family or friends through video and phone calls.
- **In the event of a medical emergency, dial 911 immediately for urgent assistance.**

STAY SAFE AFTER A PANDEMIC

Unlike most emergencies with clear beginnings and ends, a pandemic can persist for months or even years, requiring prolonged resilience and adaptability. Continue taking protective actions until it finally subsides.

Pandemics can last an extended period due to factors like the ability of viruses or bacteria to mutate and evolve, complicating the development of effective treatments or vaccines. Additionally, the spread to different regions and countries can further complicate containment efforts.

TERRORIST ATTACK

Terrorism may be perpetrated by foreign or domestic individuals or groups. When terrorists attack, their goals are usually to create mass casualties, disrupt critical resources and vital services, and to cause fear.

Acts of terrorism can be carried out using conventional means such as knives, firearms, and explosive devices including suicide bombs. Additionally, attacks may involve unconventional methods such as vehicle ramming and sophisticated approaches like airplane crashes, as well as chemical, biological, and radiological weapons.

If you notice something that doesn't seem quite right, notify local law enforcement and describe specifically what you observed:

- What you saw.
- Where you saw it.
- When you saw it.
- Why do you find it suspicious.

STAY SAFE AFTER A TERRORIST ATTACK

- If safety permits, evacuate the area immediately without stopping to retrieve your belongings or make phone calls.
- After reaching safety, contact your loved ones preferably through texting or messaging rather than phone calls.
- Follow guidance from local law enforcement.
- Stay informed by relying on credible sources of information and avoid spreading rumors that circulate on social media.
- Raw, unedited footage of terrorist events can be highly distressing, particularly for children. Exercise caution when allowing children to watch television news reports about such events. Be particularly vigilant about images and videos shared on social media.

STAY SAFE AFTER A TERRORIST ATTACK

Three primary effects typically occur: blast pressure, fragmentation, and thermal.

Blast injuries might not be visible, yet they can be serious due to internal trauma, such as organ or brain damage.

Individuals who have experienced blast injuries to the lungs may exhibit symptoms such as shortness of breath, coughing, bleeding through the natural openings of the body (nose, mouth, ears, …), chest pain, rapid breathing, and wheezing.

These symptoms could signal an internal hemorrhage which is a life-threatening condition: get some help immediately.

ACTIVE SHOOTER

An active shooter situation differs from other types of emergencies because the threat is mobile and often unpredictable.

Unlike natural disasters or stationary hazards, an active shooter moves through a populated area, targeting victims indiscriminately.

BE PREPARED FOR AN ACTIVE SHOOTER SITUATION

- Different locations, such as your school, workplace, or place of worship, may have specific plans in place for this kind of situation. Ask about these plans and familiarize yourself with them.
- If you notice something suspicious, such as people behaving oddly or using unusual communication methods, report it to local authorities.
- Be mindful of warning signs in individuals, such as expressed unusual anger, substance abuse, or intent to cause harm, as these signs may escalate over time.
- Cultivate situational awareness. Always be mindful of your surroundings and any potential dangers.
- In public places, always identify exits and hiding spots, whether you're at work, school, or special events.
- Learn lifesaving skills like first aid to assist the injured before help arrives.

111

REACT DURING AN ACTIVE SHOOTER SITUATION

Apply the "Run, Hide, Fight" strategy, used by law enforcement agencies, as a framework for responding to active shooter situations.

RUN

- If there is a safe and accessible escape route, get away from the attacker as quickly as possible.
- Encourage others to leave with you, but do not put yourself in danger by waiting for those who don't want to.
- Leave your belongings behind. Keep your empty hands raised and visible. Follow instructions from the police.
- Prevent others from entering the area.
- When you are safe and if law enforcement has not yet arrived, call 911 and provide a description of the situation.

HIDE

- If escape is not possible, find a place to hide where the shooter is less likely to find you.
- Lock and barricade doors, turn off lights, silence your phone, including vibrations, as a vibrating phone can be heard in certain conditions, and remain quiet.
- Choose a hiding spot that provides protection if shots are fired in your direction and does not trap or restrict your movement.

- Walls made of drywall typically do not provide adequate protection against fired shots. Concrete walls, steel structures, or heavy furniture offer better protection.

FIGHT

- As a last resort, and only if your life is in imminent danger, confront the shooter.
- Act aggressively, use teamwork and surprise if possible, and utilize any available objects as weapons.
- If you are able, help the wounded reach safety and provide immediate care. Prioritize your own safety first; if you are injured, you might not be able to help anyone. Call 911 when it is safe for you to do so.

STAY SAFE AFTER AN ACTIVE SHOOTER SITUATION

- Keep your hands raised and clearly visible, follow all police instructions and evacuate in the direction they indicate.
- Understand that law enforcement's primary task is to stop the shooter, and they may have to pass by injured individuals to do so.
- Consider seeking professional help for you and your family to cope with the long-term effects of trauma.

CROWD SAFETY

Regardless of your size or strength, once caught in a crowd, you lose all control.

In such circumstances, the overwhelming force of the crowd dictates your movements, emphasizing the importance of crowd safety measures and awareness in densely populated environments.

BE PREPARED FOR A CROWED EVENT

- Check the timing and agenda of the event.
- Check the event location on map, identify entry and exit points, including emergency exits.
- Avoid loose clothing or accessories that could become tangled.
- Wear closed-toe shoes and keep the laces tied.
- If you are within a group, dress your group alike or use visible color clothing.
- If the event occurs at night or indoors, prepare a mini keychain led flashlight, choose a specific color to identify your group members.
- Identify a meeting place with your group if you become separated.
- Keep your phone charged and on. Program it to vibrate and place it in a front pocket to make sure you will feel the vibrations.
- Choose a purse with a zipper and a strap (not too loose) that hangs across your body keeping your purse in front of you.

114

BE SAFE DURING A CROWDED EVENT

PREVENT

- Avoid standing on or by structures that could potentially fall or collapse.
- Leave early to avoid the rush when the event is over or wait until later.
- Stay on the side of the crowd rather than in the middle.
- To deter pickpockets: carry id, cash, and credit cards in your front pockets. Simple tip: wrap a large rubber band around your wallet, it will be more difficult to remove from your pocket.
- Have a face-mask and hand sanitizer or wipes with you.
- Make sure every member of your family is carrying a whistle around their neck (with a safety lanyard that will break-away if caught on something).

REACT

- Be aware of your surroundings, if you feel that the crowd seems to be getting out of control, leave right away (screaming, smoke, crowd movement, fights, gunshots or explosions).
- If you are caught in a moving crowd, work your way out by walking diagonally across it, never walk towards oncoming crowds.
- In an out-of-control crowd, walk with your arms around your face, elbows in front to protect your head, leaving enough space in between so you can see.

KEEPING KIDS SAFE IN CROWDED PLACES

- If your children are old enough, talk with them about where you are going, and about what they should do if something goes wrong. Give examples like if you become separated.
- Make a plan to regroup at an accessible and distinctive spot (easy to remember and to identify), or to stay put if they get lost.
- Teach them what kind of person to look for and to ask for help: another mom (a woman with kids), someone in uniform (police officer or firefighter).
- Have them remember their full name and yours (other than "mommy" and "daddy").
- Dress your kids in easily identifiable and easy to describe clothing, prefer bright colors that stand out.
- Right before leaving for the event, take a photo of your kids with your cell phone. It is much easier to show people around you, security, and law enforcement a photo of them with what they are wearing that day than it is to describe them at a time when stress will be peeking.
- Make sure they carry your phone number: on a bracelet, necklace, on their clothes tags, written on their forearm (you can even use Liquid Band-Aid to put on top of it so it doesn't smear off with sweat or rain), personalized temporary tattoos or a piece of paper with your information in their pocket (preferably laminated).

CHEMICAL AND HAZARDOUS MATERIAL

Chemicals can pose health risks under specific conditions, there are three primary ways you may come into contact with a chemical:

- **Inhalation:** breathing in the chemical.
- **Ingestion:** consuming contaminated food, water, or medication.
- **Skin contact:** touching the chemical directly or indirectly through contaminated clothing or objects.

Note that chemical exposure can occur even if you don't notice any unusual odors or visible signs, making awareness and caution crucial.

CHEMICAL ACCIDENTS AT HOME

- In case of poisoning, quickly locate the chemical container and bring it with you to the phone.
- **Immediately call the Poison Control Center (1-800-222-1222), EMS, or 911 for guidance.** Follow their instructions carefully, as the First Aid advice on the container may not be suitable.
- Do not attempt to give the person anything by mouth until medical professionals have advised you to do so.

117

CHEMICAL AND HAZARDOUS MATERIALS EMERGENCIES

Chemicals and Hazardous Materials (HazMat) incidents refer to unexpected events or accidents involving hazardous materials, such as:

- Chemical spills or leaks.
- Explosions or fires involving hazardous materials.
- Accidental releases of toxic substances.
- Transportation accidents involving hazardous materials.
- Industrial accidents or plant failures.
- Natural disasters affecting hazardous materials storage or production facilities.
- Intentional releases, such as terrorist attacks or sabotage.

Warning signs of a chemical release may include:

- Respiratory difficulties.
- Eye irritation.
- Loss of coordination.
- Nausea.
- Burning sensations in the nose, throat, and lungs.
- Additionally, a mass die-off of insects or birds in a specific area could indicate the release of a chemical agent.

STAY SAFE DURING CHEMICAL AND HAZARDOUS MATERIALS EMERGENCIES

- Follow instructions from authorities and emergency
- responders carefully, as they may have specific guidance based on the type of chemical and level of risk involved.
- Remember that some toxic chemicals are odorless and not visible.
- Stay informed by tuning into emergency broadcast stations on radio and TV.
- If authorities instruct you to "shelter in place", take immediate action to protect yourself and your loved ones.
- Gather family members and pets and move to your dedicated safe room, and:
  - Get your family emergency kit.
  - Close as many interior doors as possible.
  - Close all windows and vents.
  - Seal all windows and doors with duct tape and plastic sheeting to prevent outside air from entering.
  - Turn off all fans, heating, and cooling systems.
- If you are instructed to evacuate, leave your home quickly (evacuation bullet points).
- Depending on the type of emergency, do not drink tap water until local authorities have declared it safe for consumption.
- Avoid eating or drinking any food or water that may have been exposed to contamination.

DECONTAMINATION

If you're exposed to a chemical agent and medical help is not readily available, decontamination is the best course of action. Here are some steps to take:

- Remove contaminated clothing and personal items. Cut off clothing that is normally removed over the head, to avoid contact with the face.
- Place contaminated clothing, shoes, and other items into a plastic bag. Seal the bag tightly and label it as "Contaminated" or "Hazardous" to alert others.
- Likewise, place towels or cleaning cloths you have used in a sealed and labeled plastic bag.
- Remove eyeglasses or contact lenses immediately.
- If you wear glasses, place them in a pan of household bleach (5.25% sodium hypochlorite) for at least 30 minutes to decontaminate them, rinse the glasses thoroughly with water and dry them with a clean cloth.
- If you wear contact lenses, discard them.
- Wash exposed skin and hair with soap and water.
- Flush eyes and mouth with water.
- If helping someone decontaminate, wash your hands immediately afterwards to minimize the risk of secondary exposure.

Once you have taken initial decontamination steps and it is safe to do so, promptly seek medical attention at a nearby facility for further screening, treatment, and professional care.

RADIATION EMERGENCY

Different types of radiation emergencies include:

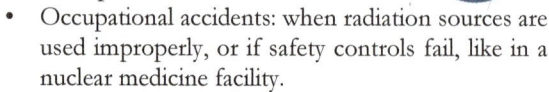

- Transportation accidents.
- Occupational accidents: when radiation sources are used improperly, or if safety controls fail, like in a nuclear medicine facility.
- Nuclear power plant accident: accidental release of radiation over an area.
- Nuclear explosion: which produces an intense pulse of heat, light, air pressure, and radiation.
- Dirty Bomb: a mix of explosives, such as dynamite, with radioactive powder or pellets.

Proximity to extremely high levels of radiation, like an atomic explosion, can lead to severe acute health effects, including skin burns and radiation sickness. Additionally, long-term exposure can increase the risk of cancer and cardiovascular disease. On the other hand, low-level environmental radiation exposure does not cause immediate health issues but contributes minimally to our overall cancer risk.

PREPARE FOR A RADIATION EMERGENCY

- Sign up for community alerts from your local emergency management agency.
- Stay informed by having multiple ways to receive alerts including a battery-powered or hand crank radio on hand, which will continue to provide vital information even if other forms of communication fail.
- Exercise caution when encountering rumors and misinformation circulating on social media.
- Build an emergency kit including a spare change of clothes for each family member, trash bags to contain contaminated clothing, a sharpie to label the bag as "Contaminated", sealed supplies of water, food, and medicine.

STAY SAFE DURING A RADIATION EMERGENCY

- Apply the fundamental principles of radiation protection: time, distance, and shielding. Minimize your exposure time, maximize your distance from the radiation source, and seek shelter in a sturdy building.
- If a radiation hazard warning is issued, seek immediate shelter inside the nearest building. Move to a room or area with minimal windows and put as many walls and barriers as possible between you and the outside to maximize protection from external radiation.

NUCLEAR EXPLOSION

- **If the detonation occurs on the ground, it can lift material into the air, creating a cloud of dangerous, sand-like particles called fallout, which are radioactive and can contaminate the environment.**

- Seek immediate cover from the blast behind any available shelter. If you're outside, lie face down to protect your skin from the intense heat and flying debris. Once the shockwave passes, quickly enter the nearest building for safety.

- Substantial barriers like lead, concrete, or water offer protection against radiation.

- Following a nuclear detonation, you have a critical 10-minute window or more to seek adequate shelter before the fallout arrives. Opt for buildings with sturdy brick or concrete walls, or underground facilities. Turn off all fans, air conditioners, and forced-air heating units that draw in outside air, seal all windows and doors to prevent air leaks, close fireplace dampers to prevent outside air from entering. Bring pets and service animals inside to keep them safe.

- Stay indoors for at least 24 hours after the detonation, unless you face an immediate danger like a fire, gas leak, building collapse, or severe injury. Radiation levels drop significantly and become less hazardous within the first 24 hours, making it crucial to wait for the all-clear from authorities before exiting your shelter.

- Don't consume unsealed foods from outside, including garden produce as they may be contaminated with radioactive material.
- Remove your outer layer of clothing to decontaminate yourself and reduce radioactive material on your body. This simple step can eliminate up to 90% of radioactive material. Be cautious when removing your clothing to prevent radioactive dust from spreading and avoid touching your face, especially your eyes, nose, and mouth, to minimize exposure.

POTASSIUM IODIDE

Potassium iodide (KI) is a type of salt, similar to table salt, that is commonly added to make it "iodized." If taken promptly and in the right amount, potassium iodide can prevent the thyroid gland from absorbing radioactive iodine, which could reduce the risk of thyroid cancer and other related diseases that might result from exposure to radioactive iodine released during a severe nuclear accident.

 You should only take potassium iodide if explicitly instructed to do so by local public health authorities, emergency management officials, or your healthcare provider. Potassium iodide is not a general anti-radiation drug.

DECONTAMINATION

- If you're exposed to radiation dust, here are some decontamination steps to take:
- Remove contaminated clothing and personal items. Cut off clothing that is normally removed over the head, to avoid contact with the face.
- Place contaminated clothing, shoes, and other items into a plastic bag. Seal the bag and label it as "Contaminated" or "Hazardous" to alert others.
- Likewise, place towels or cleaning cloths you have used in a sealed and labeled plastic bag.
- Remove eyeglasses or contact lenses immediately.
- If you wear glasses, place them in a pan of household bleach (5.25% sodium hypochlorite) for at least 30 minutes to decontaminate them, rinse the glasses thoroughly with water and dry them with a clean cloth.
- If you wear contact lenses, discard them.
- Wash exposed skin and hair with soap and water.
- Flush eyes and mouth with water.
- If helping someone decontaminate, wash your hands immediately afterwards to minimize the risk of secondary exposure.
- If your pets were outside when the radioactive dust arrived, gently brush their coat to remove any loose particles, and wash them with soap and water.
- Once you have taken initial decontamination steps and it is safe to do so, promptly seek medical attention at a nearby facility for further screening, treatment, and professional care.

EQUIPPED

EMERGENCY KIT

CONSIDER 3 TYPES OF EMERGENCY KITS

- **Family Emergency Kit (Home)** ready to sustain your household for at least a week in the event of a disaster. This kit should include necessities tailored to your family's needs. Have it readily accessible, so it can be quickly grabbed and used during an emergency. In the event of an evacuation, have a portable emergency kit that can easily be transported in your car.

- **Car Emergency Kit (One for Each Vehicle)** for ensuring preparedness while on the move. These kits should contain items, tools, and supplies to sustain you and your passengers for at least 24 hours in case of roadside emergencies or unexpected delays. Having them readily available ensures quick access during emergencies.

- **Mini Emergency Kit (Personal Carry)** for ensuring personal safety and readiness in various situations. This kit should contain essential items tailored to your individual needs and daily activities. Ensure it's ready to grab and use at a moment's notice, whether you're commuting, traveling, or engaging in outdoor activities.

 Emergency kits must be tailored to your specific needs.

127

ANATOMY OF AN EMERGENCY BAG

- During times of high stress, you'll rely heavily on the robustness of your emergency kit and its various components: handles, shoulder straps, pockets, and zippers.
- Keep in mind that you'll need to carry your bag, so it should be durable yet lightweight and practical.
- Opt for bags with light-colored interiors to facilitate visibility and quick item retrieval.
- Each item should be stored in a designated compartment within your emergency bag, enabling easy access even in low-light conditions or moments of high stress and confusion.
- External attachments such as gear loops, loading straps, or MOLLE systems (Modular Lightweight Load-carrying Equipment, originally designed for military tactical bags) are invaluable for securing items outside your bag for swift access.
- Consider adding a reflective strip to your bag if it lacks one to enhance visibility, particularly in low-light environments.

THE GOLDEN RULES FOR EMERGENCY KITS

- Store it in an easily accessible place; your portable kit should be positioned by an exit.
- Make sure all individuals in your emergency plan know the kit's location and contents.
- Ensure familiarity with the use of each item in your emergency kits.
- Ensure every item is readily usable by avoiding excess packaging.
- Regularly check and update/replenish kit items as necessary. Tip: Set reminders in your electronic calendar.
- Prioritize quality over trendy items based on your budget.

EMERGENCY KIT ITEMS

ITEMS CATEGORY 1: EQUIPMENT AND TOOLS

Selected according to your personal needs and living environment.

- Multitool: an indispensable tool for various tasks and repairs.
- Flashlights (with extra batteries): essential for illumination during power outages or nighttime emergencies, with one per person.
- Duct tape: versatile for patching, sealing, fixing, and repairing various items, ensure at least 10 feet.
- Paracord: a lightweight and durable nylon rope useful for various purposes, provide at least 20 feet.
- Emergency whistle: a signaling device for attracting attention in emergencies, with one per person.
- Mirror: useful for emergency signaling and personal hygiene checks in case of injury.
- Sewing kit: includes needles, thread, and patches for repairing clothing and gear.
- Solar power charger: provides a renewable energy source for charging electronic devices.
- Compass: even a basic compass can aid in orienting yourself in unfamiliar terrain.
- Printed local maps: essential for navigation, especially in areas with limited or no cell service.

 Each item should be selected according to your personal needs and living environment.

ITEMS CATEGORY 2: PROTECTIVE GEAR

- Emergency blanket: provides warmth and insulation in cold conditions.
- Reflective band: enhances visibility for safety, especially in low-light conditions.
- Rain poncho: protects against rain and moisture to maintain dryness.
- Light hat or cap: provides sun protection and shields against elements.
- Sunglasses: protects eyes from harmful UV rays and glare.
- 100% Cotton scarf: versatile for various uses, such as bandaging or protection against dust.
- N95 face-mask: provides respiratory protection against dust and other airborne particles.
- Work gloves: protects hands during cleanup and handling of debris.
- Goggles: shields eyes from dust, debris, and potential hazards.
- Ensure that you have one of these items per person and that they fit correctly. These items should be unpacked and prepared for immediate use in case of emergencies.

ITEMS CATEGORY 3: FIRST AID

- Adhesive bandages: 10 small, 15 medium, 5 large.
- Gauze dressing pads (4x4 inches): 10 pieces
- Antiseptic cleansing wipes: 4 wipes
- Triangular bandage: 1 piece
- Gauze roll bandage (3 inches): 1 roll
- First aid tape roll: 1 roll
- Latex-free vinyl gloves: 2 pairs
- Tylenol (500mg): 2 tablets
- Benadryl (25mg): 4 tablets
- EMT shears: 1 pair
- Stainless steel tweezers: 1 pair
- Hand sanitizer

According to Personal and Family Needs:

- Specific medications + copies of prescriptions
- Epinephrine auto-injector: 1 device

Optional (for trained personnel):

- Trauma gauze (hemostatic dressing) (3x24 inches): 1 piece
- CPR one-way valve face shield (latex-free): 1 piece
- CAT (Combat Action Tourniquet) tourniquet + sharpie: 1 set

 If you are uncertain about the symptoms of a victim or in case of emergency, call 911.

ITEMS CATEGORY 4: FOOD AND WATER

When stocking up on food for emergency preparedness, prioritize items with a long shelf life that don't require refrigeration. Ensure these items provide adequate nutrition by considering **daily calorie needs:**

- Adult women: 1,600 to 2,400 calories/day.
- Adult men: 2,000 to 3,000 calories/day.
- Young children: 1,000 to 2,000 calories/day (varies by age, weight, and activity level).

Include sources of protein, carbohydrates, and healthy fats to sustain energy levels. Avoid salty snacks that increase thirst and the need for water. Opt for tasty foods you enjoy maintaining morale during challenging times.

Water is vital for health, with individual needs varying based on factors like physical condition, weight, activity level, and weather conditions.
As a general guideline:

- Men: about 15.5 cups (3.7 liters) per day.
- Women: about 11.5 cups (2.7 liters) per day.
- Children: 6 to 8 cups (1.5 to 2 liters) per day (varies by age).

While 20 to 25 percent of daily fluid intake typically comes from other beverages and food, water remains the best choice. Always prioritize water consumption to ensure hydration, especially during emergencies.

ITEMS CATEGORY 5: DOCUMENTS AND COMMUNICATION

Your communication plan should facilitate communication in scenarios where mobile network and Internet access are either available or unavailable.

- Writing tools and materials: sharpie, pencil, and waterproof notebook for recording important information.
- Secured flash drive: contains essential documents such as IDs, insurance papers, birth certificates, etc. (check the "Essential documents" chapter for a comprehensive list).
- Paper copies: contact information, personal emergency plan, emergency communication strategy, and evacuation checklists.
- Local paper maps: essential for navigating evacuation routes in case of emergencies.
- Phone charger: ensure your phone charger is readily available and fully charged.
- Radio: battery-powered, solar, or hand-crank radio with extra batteries for receiving emergency broadcasts.
- Cash: small bills for purchasing essential items or services in case of emergencies.

 Ensure you're familiar with radio frequencies for emergency broadcasts, as accessing them may be challenging without Internet or mobile networks. Program or note these frequencies on your radio beforehand.

ITEMS CATEGORY 6: HYGIENE AND COMFORT

Maintaining hygiene and finding comfort during disaster situations is crucial for both physical and mental well-being.

Hygiene Items:

- Soap for handwashing and general cleanliness.
- Baby wipes for personal hygiene and cleaning purposes.
- Toothbrush and toothpaste for oral hygiene.
- Personal hygiene items such as feminine hygiene products or razors.
- Garbage bags for waste disposal and maintaining cleanliness.

Comfort Items:

- Favorite books for relaxation and distraction.
- Little toys or stuffed animals for children to provide comfort and entertainment.
- Card games and crayons for family bonding and amusement.
- Meaningful family photos and videos stored on your phone or dedicated device to provide emotional support and connection during difficult times.

Including these items in your emergency kit ensures you can maintain hygiene standards and find moments of comfort and solace during challenging circumstances.

PET EMERGENCY KIT

DON'T FORGET ABOUT THEM!

Ensure their safety by preparing an emergency kit tailored to their needs:

- Food: Pack a supply for several days, including treats.
- Water: Store enough water to meet their needs.
- Medication: Have extra supplies of any regular medications your pet requires.
- Traveling Gear: Include a bag, crate, or sturdy carrier along with a leash.
- Sanitation and Grooming: Include newspapers, paper towels, wipes, and trash bags.
- Identification: Attach a collar with an ID tag and include copies of registration information and relevant documents.
- Photo: Keep a picture of you and your pet together in case of separation.
- Comfort Items: Include favorite toys and familiar objects to help reduce stress.
- Instructions: Prepare a note with care instructions in case you need to entrust your pet to someone else.

By assembling these items, you can ensure your pets' safety and well-being during emergencies.

CELL PHONE TIPS

SAVE YOUR CELL PHONE BATTERY

- Reduce the brightness of your screen.
- Turn off wifi, bluetooth or cell network according to your needs and situation.
- Turn off any background apps according to your needs and situation.
- Turn off location services if you are safe at home.
- Have a charged, external battery ready.
- Avoid exposing your phone to temperatures higher than 95°F (35°C).
- Remove case if device gets warm while charging.

EMERGENCY MESSAGING

- Text messages use less bandwidth than calls. Moreover, even if the message can't get through right away because networks are overwhelmed, it might be delayed but sent.
- Keep it short and accurate: time, status, location, intent, signature (in case you are not using your own phone).
- Start your message with the current time (your message might be delayed because of a connection issue).

  Example: *01:30 pm, I am safe at home with mom, we are staying here. Scott*

- Use an out-of-town contact as a relay (this person must be included in your emergency plan and briefed accordingly).

BASIC RULES TO STAY WARM

Cover each part of your body appropriately, especially your head, face, mouth, chest, abdomen, hands, and feet.

Stay dry: wet clothing chills the body quickly, sweating will cause your body to lose more heat.

Shivering signals your body is losing heat; it is its way of warming up by rapidly tightening and relaxing muscles.

Apply the three layers system to stay warm and to regulate comfort by slipping layers on and off according to the weather changes and to your activity level.

INNER LAYER: WARM AND DRY

The first layer should keep your body warm and dry, it should be made of fabric that doesn't absorb moisture. This layer requires a snug fit to wick sweat efficiently. Prefer polypropylene (synthetic), wool or silk rather than cotton.

MIDDLE LAYER: INSULATION

The insulation layer will retain heat by trapping air close to your body, it should be well fitted but not tight. Primary fabric choices are: wool, goose down, or polyester fleece.

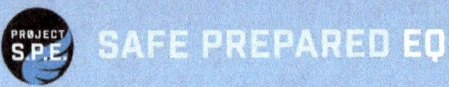
OUTER LAYER: WIND AND RAIN PROTECTION

The outermost layer must protect you from wind, rain, and snow. It can be waterproof or water-resistant, depending on the rain condition, but needs to be a breathable shield. These clothes are usually made of polyester fabrics.

ESSENTIAL KNOTS

SQUARE KNOT

Use: to quickly and easily tie two ends of a single line together. It can be used to tie a bandage around a wound, to secure a triangular bandage or a splint.

Caution: This knot is not suitable for critical safety situations, due to its ease of unraveling.

Instructions:
1. Cross right over left.
2. Take right under left.
3. Cross right over left again.
4. Pull to tighten.

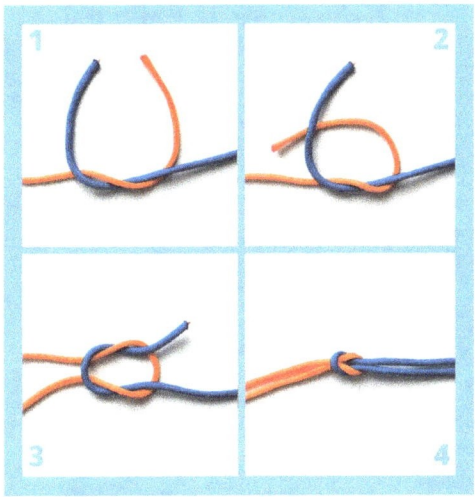

BOWLINE KNOT

Use: To make a secure loop that will not slip or bind under load. It creates a secure, fixed loop, it will not slip or jam, it is easy to tie and untie.

Instructions:
1. Create a small loop.
2. Pass working end through loop.
3. Pass working around standing part.
4. Pass working end through loop.
5. Pull to tighten.

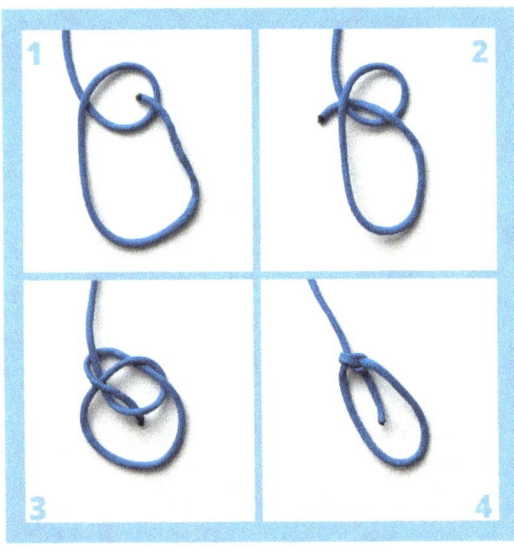

TAUTLINE KNOT

Use: To make an adjustable loop that can be slipped to tighten or loosen a line. It's easy to adjust, it maintains tension, it allows for quick length adjustments.

How it works: the Tautline Knot creates a movable loop that slides along the standing part of the rope, adjusting tension.

Instructions:
1. Wrap rope around post/object.
2. Pass working end under standing part.
3. Make 3-4 turns around standing part.
4. Pass working end through loop.
5. Pull to tighten.

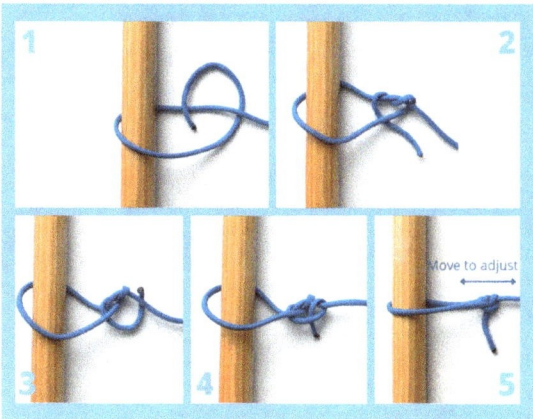

142

MOORING HITCH

Use: Use: To temporarily tie an object. It can be released quickly with a pull of the free end.

Caution: This is not a secure knot.

Instructions: 1. Wrap rope around post/object.
2. Form a loop and pull a section of the standing line through your loop.
3. Pull a section of the free end through the new loop.
4. Pull the standing line to tighten.
5. Release the knot by pulling the free end.

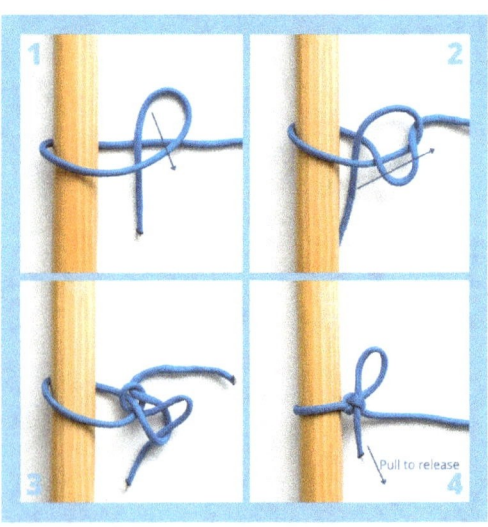

143

PARACORD

Paracord, short for "parachute cord," typically consists of a woven outer sheath and multiple inner strands, which can be unraveled and used individually for various purposes.

- Building a stretcher, a sling, an emergency rescue line.
- Strapping a handle to carry heavy items.
- Repairing equipment.
- Tying items to your backpack.
- Securing a shelter.
- Replacing your shoelaces.

You can use the internal strands as:

- Sewing kit.
- Dental floss.
- Fishing line.

Paracord comes in various thicknesses, colors, and patterns.

The different thicknesses are typically labeled as "Type" or by their breaking strength in pounds. For instance, the most commonly used "Paracord Type III" is also known as "550 Paracord" which has a breaking strength of 550 lbs (249 kg).

Paracord 550 is not made for climbing:
A falling person weighs a lot more than a static person.
The thin diameter of the paracord makes it more likely to break in case of friction.
Paracord stretches more than a climbing rope.

COMPASS

In remote areas with no phone signal or battery, a traditional compass can be a vital tool for navigation.

There are two distinct norths to consider: true north and magnetic north.

True north refers to the geographic North Pole, while magnetic north is the direction indicated by the Earth' magnetic field. The difference between true north and magnetic north, which can vary depending on your location, is called the "declination" or "variation".

When you're navigating in the wilds, or unfamiliar terrain, it's important to accurately adjust for declination. Even an error of just one degree can result in a significant deviation of 100 feet per mile.

Although the declination value can be located on a topographic map, it's crucial to verify the map's revision date since this value changes over time.

Once you have determined the declination value, apply it to your bearings by adding or subtracting the value as needed: **east declination is represented by positive numbers, while west declination is represented by negative numbers, apply this rule consistently in your calculations.**

COMPASS

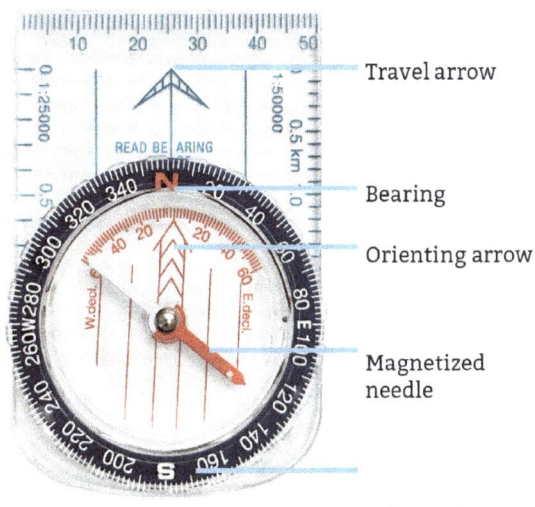

Travel arrow

Bearing

Orienting arrow

Magnetized
needle

Azimut ring

146

TRAVELING BY COMPASS WITH A MAP

1. Place your compass on the map, aligning the travel arrow with the top of the map.

2. Align the 'N' (north) marker with the direction-of-travel arrow by rotating the bezel, and don't forget to apply the declination value shown on the map to guarantee a precise match between your map and the surroundings.

3. Slide the baseplate until one of its edges aligns with either the left or right edge of the map, keeping the travel arrow pointing upwards.

4. Hold both map and compass steady, then rotate your body until the magnetic needle's tip falls within the orienting arrow's outline.

Your map is now correctly oriented, allowing you to identify nearby landmarks. Keep consulting your map along the way to stay oriented. Remember, it's always easier to stay on track than to find your way back after getting lost.

TRAVELING BY COMPASS WITHOUT A MAP

It might sound obvious but the first thing you need to do is to look around you and get familiar with your surroundings. Choose a visible landmark, such as a mountain, or building, that you want to travel towards.

2. Hold the compass in front of you with the travel arrow pointing in the direction you're heading. Ensure the compass is held level and steady.

3. Align the compass: rotate the azimuth ring until the orienting arrow aligns with the magnetic needle's red end, which points towards north.

4. Sight along the compass: read the bearing aligned with the travel arrow.

5. Keep the compass in front of you and follow the direction indicated by the direction-of-travel arrow.

6. Periodically re-orient: repeat steps 2-5 periodically to ensure you remain on course, especially if the terrain or visibility changes.

As long as you keep the red needle and the orienting arrow aligned, you'll be heading in the same direction.

EMERGENCY WHISTLE

In an emergency situation, it can get you help faster than technology. People around you will know that something is wrong.

You can signal up to one mile around you (depending on your physical environment and weather conditions).

A whistle blast is much louder than a human scream, and using it will save your voice, your energy and, in case of cold weather, your body heat.

Make sure every member of your family is carrying a whistle, attached to their backpack strap or around their neck (with a safety lanyard that will break-away if caught on something). In an emergency situation or on a hike, you or your loved ones will be able to call for help immediately.

 Three strong blows of the whistle are known as an international distress call and will be recognized by rescue teams.

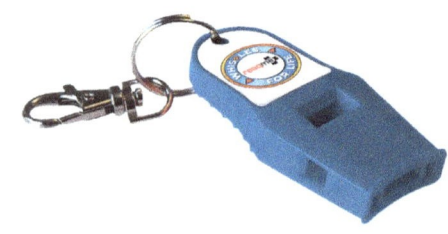

REFLECTIVE BAND

In a disaster or emergency situation, being visible to others is just as crucial as having visibility. A reflective band brightly reflects light sources, alerting others to your presence in environments or circumstances where safety may be compromised.

During situations of low visibility such as darkness, fog, dust, or rain, a reflective band becomes invaluable in enhancing your visibility. In case of evacuation or power outages, ensure that you and your family members wear reflective bands, complemented by mini flashlights to illuminate the darkness and maintain visual contact with one another.

This is especially comforting for children, as being able to see other family members serves as a source of reassurance. As a tip, consider having an extra reflective band for their favorite stuffed animal to further enhance their visibility and sense of security.

SPACE BLANKET

A space blanket has a metallic coating able to reflect up to 80% of radiated heat. Many feature a dual-sided design, with one side colored and the other side shiny and reflective.

- To keep yourself warm, wrap it over dry clothes with the shiny surface inside. Since it stops evaporation, make sure you vent it just enough to avoid vapor build-up inside the blanket (wet clothing increases heat loss by a factor of 5).

- Place it in front of a heat source, like a campfire, to reflect heat back to you but avoid contact between the blanket and any open flame.

- If trapped in your car in cold weather: cover the windows with the space blanket shiny side inside.

- Cut pieces of the space blanket to put inside your shoes or under your coat (not next to the skin). Take caution to prevent excessive sweating.

- With a double-sided space blanket, place the shiny side of the blanket outward to protect against the sun heat. Same thing for your shelter or your car.

- As a signal for help, the shiny surface of the blanket is highly visible from the sky when oriented toward rescuers or when using the reflection of your flashlight at night.

FACE-MASK

In the aftermath of a disaster such as an earthquake or wildfire, exposure to air pollutants like smoke and dust is highly probable. Furthermore, following a hurricane, tornado, or flood, the presence of excess moisture and standing water fosters the growth of mold, posing health risks. Regardless of the specific disaster, it's crucial to protect yourself with a face-mask.

Type of masks: cloth, paper mask and tissue won't protect you from smoke, you need a respirator mask that fits you to form a tight enough seal to ensure protection. N95 and KN95 respirators are rated to capture 95% of tiny particles (0.3 micron particles), 94% for the Korean KF94.

Exhalation valves on masks facilitate easier breathing and help reduce moisture buildup inside the mask. However, because the valve allows unfiltered air to escape from the mask, it is not the most suitable option for preventing the spread of contagious respiratory diseases.

Children: make sure you have respirators specifically made for children.

EMERGENCY CONTACT LIST

Family members ....

....

....

....

....

....

Friends, neighbors ....

....

....

....

....

....

Out-of-town contact ....

....

Care providers ....

....

....

Local emergency services ....

....

....

PERSONAL NOTES

....
....
....
....
....
....
....
....
....
....
....
....
....
....
....
....
....
....
....
....
....
....

PERSONAL NOTES

....
....
....
....
....
....
....
....
....
....
....
....
....
....
....
....
....
....
....
....
....

Thank you for taking the time to read this emergency preparedness guide. I hope the resources and information within these pages have empowered you to build resilience and confidence in the face of uncertainty.

If you have any comments, questions, or feedback, please don't hesitate to reach out to me at hello@projectspe.com, I'd love to hear from you.

To learn more about how Project SPE can empower you or your organization with resilience and crisis leadership skills, scan the QR code below and connect with me on LinkedIn.

Stay sharp and safe!

Franck

www.ingramcontent.com/pod-product-compliance
Lightning Source LLC
Chambersburg PA
CBHW060530130626
46553CB00002B/699